Bead Play with Fringe
Techniques, Design and Projects

Jamie Cloud Eakin

Copyright © 2014 Jamie Cloud Eakin, All rights reserved. This book may not be reproduced by any means, in part or in whole without the written permission of the author. The jewelry designs in Bead Play with Fringe are copyrighted. You may use them for your education, personal enjoyment and/or donation to a non-profit group for sale or display. Production for sales using these designs is limited to 3 per year, no mass production. They may not be taught without prior written permission.

We take great care to ensure that the information included is accurate and presented in good faith, but no warranty is provided nor are results guaranteed. Having no control over the choices of materials or procedures used or individual skills, neither the author nor publisher shall have any liability to any person or entity with respect to any loss or damage caused directly or indirectly by the information contained in this book.

Trademark ™ and registered trademark names are used through this book. Rather than use the symbols with every occurrence of a trademark or registered trademark name, we are using the names only in the editorial fashion to the benefit of the owner, with no intention of infringement.

Published by JCE Publishing
Copyright © 2014 Jamie Cloud Eakin
All rights reserved.
ISBN-10: 1500777412
ISBN-13: 978-1500777418

Contents

Introduction	4
Chapter 1 - Supplies	5
Chapter 2 - Fringe basics	8
Chapter 3 - Standard Fringe	15
Chapter 4 - Loop Fringe	36
Chapter 5 - Kinky Fringe	52
Chapter 6 - Branch Fringe	60
Chapter 7 - Twisted and Spiral Fringes	77
Chapter 8 – Basic Procedures	87
Index	93
About the Author	93
Acknowledgements	94

Introduction

Beads … beads…. Beads! Often the best case is *the more the merrier* and there is nothing like adding beaded fringe to create the maximum "WOW" effect. The addition of fringe can take a simple design and make it spectacular or take a complex design to a whole new level. Fringe techniques are perfect for finishing your designs with flair and panache.

While designers will find the information that follows extremely valuable, all beaders will benefit. Too often, projects simply instruct to "add fringe" and while the thread path is shown, a full understanding of the construction of fringe is simply not covered; but you will find that here along with many helpful tips. With this book, you can improve your technical abilities and begin to confidently add fringe to any design.

There are many fringe techniques, and each has its own personality. First I'll catalogue the varieties and illustrate how to create them. This will help you not only in creating the fabulous projects, but it will provide a resource and reference anytime you are creating fringe.

The projects show you how to create fabulous jewelry while you learn the process and perfect your technique. So get out those beads and let the fun flow!

Chapter 1: Supplies

Supplies:

Seed Beads

Seed beads, small glass beads named for the seeds they resemble, are used throughout the projects. Seed beads are sized according to number, the higher the number the smaller the bead. The most commonly used size is size 11/0 (aka size 11). There are essentially two types of seed beads. One type is a cylinder bead and includes Delicas and Tohos. These beads are straight on the sides and on the hole edges (a cylindrical shape) and have large holes. The other type is a rocaille which is more round in shape. Within the realm of rocailles, the most popular are Japanese seed beads and Czech seed beads. Japanese beads tend to have a larger hole than Czech beads and tend to be longer in length. Cylinder beads and Japanese rocailles are sold by the gram while Czech beads are generally sold by the hank.

Tip: The supplies lists show the number of grams needed. If you are using Czech beads which are sold by the hank, you need to convert to grams. One hank of size 11/0 beads is approximately 36 grams.

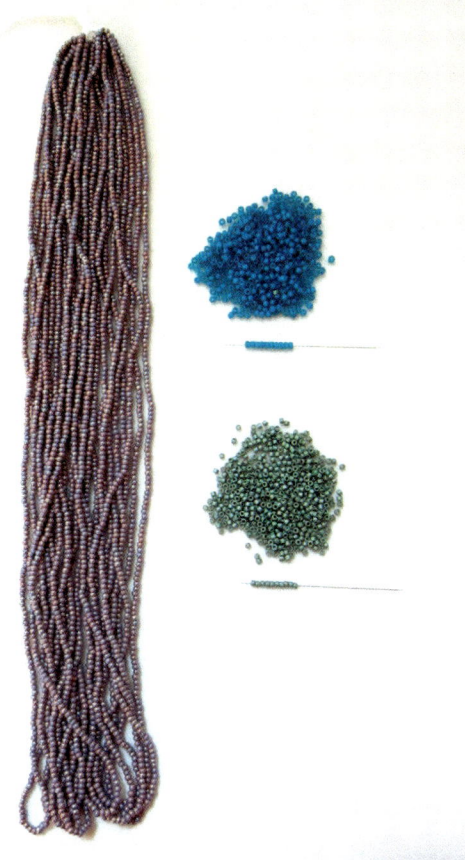

Czech hank (left), Japanese (top right) and Delicas (bottom right)

This is how beads are sized (lined up hole side up, not strung). There are ten (10) beads in each row. Note that Japanese (top) and Czech (middle) rocailles are the same while Delicas (bottom) are smaller.

Tip: Read Culling Beads on page 87.

There are fifteen (15) beads in each row but the result is different lengths from the different types of beads. Top: Japanese rocailles, Middle: Czech rocailles, Bottom Delicas

The projects use rocailles because the rounded edges with the smaller holes make it easier to achieve the proper tension in the fringe. The tension needs to be loose enough for a bendable flow in the fringe and also tight enough so there is not a gap allowing the thread to show.

Rocailles line up better so getting a proper tension is easier. Even though creating fringe is easier using rocailles, you can use any type of seed bead in fringe. When you are selecting beads to add fringe to a design, the bead choice is typically influenced by the beads used in the rest of the beadwork. You may want to use Delicas or another type of cylinder bead particularly when that is the type of bead used in the beadwork. The primary issue with using these beads in fringe is that the larger holes make lining up the beads more difficult. Use doubled thread to fill up the larger holes so that the beads line up easier and better.

Other Beads

Beads are made of many different materials including glass, crystal, genuine stone, shell or anything that can have a hole drilled into it. There are many shapes of beads and the variety of shapes provides interesting opportunities for fringe design. As a general rule, the bead hole is drilled into the center of a bead. However there are many beads with the hole drilled in another position shown in the photos (right).

Needles

Beading needles are different from regular sewing needles, and are much thinner. They are made specifically for beading and will be labeled as "beading needles". Beading needles are sized by number (such as 10, 12, 13, and up) the higher the number, the smaller the needle. Needles also come in different lengths; the standard is a 2 inch needle. Long needles, 4 inches and up, are also available and are necessary when stitching through very long beads. Shorter needles, referred to as Sharps, are also commonly used by many beaders. When creating fringe, a standard 2 inch needle is recommended.
When beading with size 11/0 seed beads, the favorite needle size to use is a size 12. If you only want to stock one size needle in your stash, that is the recommended size. Another way to view needles is that they are a "tool" and having a variety of sizes including 10, 12 and 13 is useful. A size 10 needle is easier to thread and hold so use it to start projects. The added advantage of using a larger needle is that it will help cull out any beads with small holes since the needle won't easily fit. This is especially helpful when later steps call for stitching through the beads again. Switch to a Size 12 needle when you perform the latter steps. Have some size 13 needles available to use when you need to stitch through a bead again, but it is too tight for a size 12 needle. Replacing the needle to change the size is easy when working with single thread. If a process calls for doubled thread, just use the smaller size needle (size 12) since you can't change the needle as you bead.

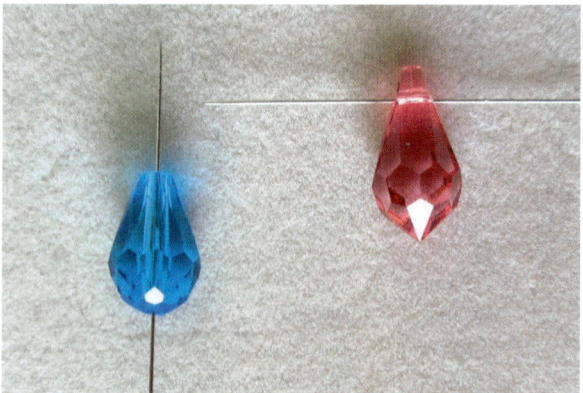
Center drilled teardrop (left), Top-drilled teardrop (right)

Center drilled leaf (left), Top drilled leaf (Center), Top and side drilled leaf (right)

Thread

Beading thread comes in various colors and is generally made from nylon (like Nymo or Sono or Silamide) and may be pre-waxed. Beading threads are stronger than threads made for sewing which should not be used. The choice of beading thread, whether it's Nymo, Silamide or a similar thread product, is often a personal preference and each is satisfactory. Threads are sized with an alphabetic designation such as A, B, C, etc.
There are other products used for beading such as Fireline, and Power Pro that are woven or braided fibers

of polyethylene. Because of the way these threads are constructed, fringe made with these threads does not have the same supple movement as with the other threads. So, even if you choose to use those threads for other parts of the construction of beadwork, it is recommended that you switch to Nymo, Silamide, or another fiber type of thread for the fringe work.

Tools

Tools are used often in creating beadwork and are available in most bead and/or crafts stores and on the internet.

Beading Pad

Made specifically for beading, these pads are like a fleece blanket with a nap like that of velvet. The pad provides a cushion that allows you to pour out small piles of beads that stay in place without rolling around. The beads sit on top of the fibers and are easy to pick up with a needle.

Findings

"Findings" is a jewelry term used to describe the hardware used in jewelry creations such as clasps, jump rings, head pins, etc. Most bead stores carry a vast variety of such hardware in metals ranging from inexpensive plated brass to more costly sterling silver, gold-filled and gold.

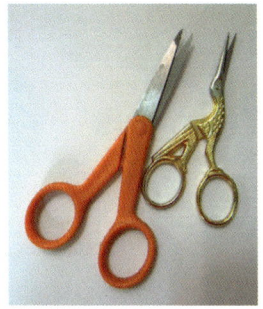
Scissors

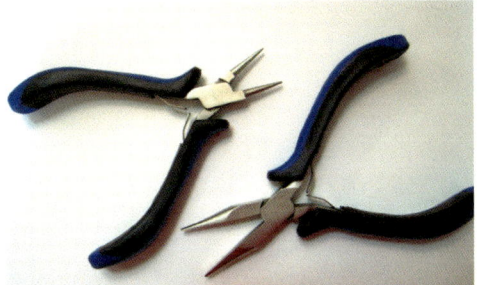
Round nose and Needle nose pliers

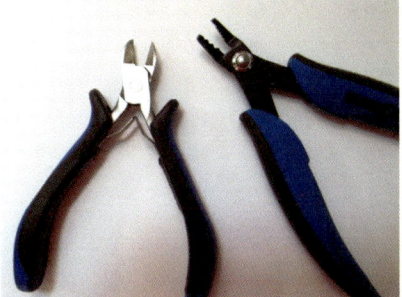
Side Cutters and Crimp Tool

Scissors

Scissors with sharp blades and a small size for easy handling are an essential part of a beading tool chest.

Pliers

You need two sets of pliers in your beading tool chest; one type is Needle Nose and the other type is Round Nose. Pliers are used to attach findings to beadwork. Use one in each hand to open and close a jump ring. Use the round nose pliers to shape head pins or wire into a circle/loop. If you are purchasing these from a hardware store, be sure to get small sizes that are easy to handle.

Wire Cutters/Crimp Tool

It is often necessary to trim the length of a head pin or other wires. Wire cutters known as Side Cutters are a perfect tool for these purposes. While you can squeeze a crimp bead with Needle nose pliers, investing in a Crimp tool is preferred. The crimp tool has two sections: one to initially press the crimp bead around the wire and a second to fold the pressed crimp bead into a small rounder formation. These are also useful to use when you choose to add a crimp cover over the crimp bead.

Clasps

Clasps are findings that provide a mechanism to open and close necklaces and bracelets. There are many styles and types such as hook and eye, hook and chain, toggle, spring ring, magnetic, etc. Most types are suitable for all uses and the choice becomes one of personal preference. However, hook and eye type of clasps should not be used for bracelets.

Jump Rings

Jump rings are small wire circles use to join beadwork to some other kind of finding such as a clasp. The ring has a slit on it that can be opened. You open the ring, insert it through the loop on the clasp and the loop on the beadwork and then close the ring. Be careful not to open the jump ring by spreading the ends outward and enlarging the circle; you'll weaken the ring and destroy the roundness. Instead, using a pair of pliers in each hand, twist the ring open pushing one end forward and the other end backward. Close in the same manner, reversing the direction.

Chapter 2: Fringe basics

There are two technical aspects for adding fringe to beadwork. First is the construction of the fringe and second is how to attach it to beadwork.

Construction of the fringe

There are many types of fringe, each with its own unique look, challenges and design opportunities. Below are the pictures of the types of fringe with a reference to find detailed information about its construction and design.

Standard Fringe
Page 15

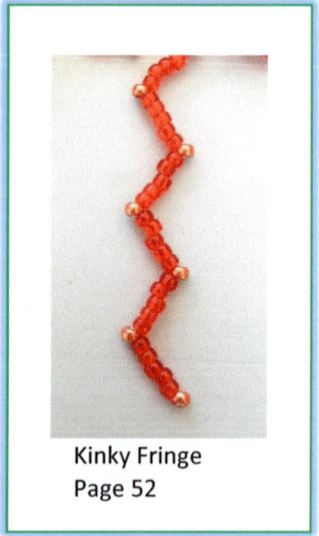

Kinky Fringe
Page 52

Branch Fringe
Page 60

Circles Branch
Page 63

Loop Branch
Page 63

8

Loop Fringe
Page 36

Twisted Fringe
Page 77

Twisted Variation
Page 77

Spiral Fringe
Page 80

Ribbon Spiral
Page 83

Ribbon Spiral
Smoothed Page 83

Fringe Ends:

Standard Turn Bead End
Page 10

Picot End
Page 10

Star End
Page 10

Leaf End
Page 11

Loop End
Page 11

The function of the end bead(s) is to hold the other beads on the thread. There are a variety of techniques so you can choose a method that is best for your fringe design.

Standard Turn Bead End

A Standard Turn Bead End is the easiest and most popularly used technique. This is the last bead picked up to create a fringe strand and is typically a 15/0 or 11/0 seed bead. The key criteria to consider when selecting a turn bead is that it needs to be larger than the hole in the bead above it. If that hole is larger than the desired turn bead, consider using a bead cap or rondelle bead to reduce the size of the hole. Alternatively, you need to select a larger turn bead or the fringe beads will fall off.

1. Pick up the beads for the fringe strands and last, pick up the turn bead.

2. Skip the turn bead and stitch back up the fringe strand.

3. Hold and pull the turn bead with one hand and pull on the thread with the other hand to adjust the tension.

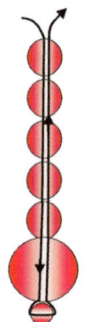 

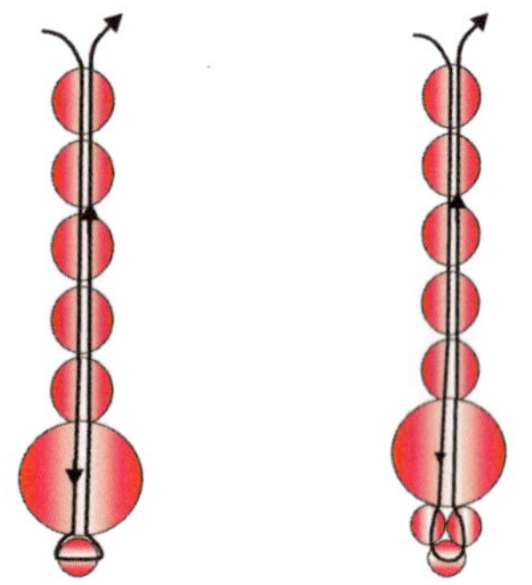

Standard Turn Bead   Picot End

Picot End

The Picot end is similar to a Standard Turn Bead but is a group of three beads typically 11/0 or 15/0 seed beads. Like a Standard Turn Bead, the size of these beads need to be larger than the hole in the final bead, not just as a group but individually. If the strand gets pulled, the picot can move and one bead can slip into the hole. When that happens, the beads will fall off the fringe strand. You can prevent this by using the proper size beads - the first and last beads of the picot trio must each be larger than the bead hole of the last bead.

1. Pick up the beads for the fringe strand and last, pick up three beads for the Picot End.

2. Skip the three beads for the Picot End and stitch back up the fringe strand.

3. Hold and pull the middle bead in the picot with one hand and pull on the thread with the other hand to adjust the tension.

Star End

This end is stitched at the bottom of the fringe typically with 15/0 beads but 11/0 beads can be used. This process takes much more time than the other fringe ends but has a stunning (and well worth it) effect.

1. Pick up the beads for the fringe strand plus eleven seed beads and move to the bottom of the fringe strand. Stitch through the first seed bead again creating a circle and pull the thread to adjust the tension. Stitch through the circle again and through the first added bead. Pull to adjust the tension in the fringe strand again.

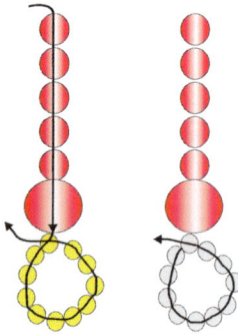

2. Pick up five seed beads. Skip the next bead in the circle and stitch through the next bead. Repeat around the circle to the top.

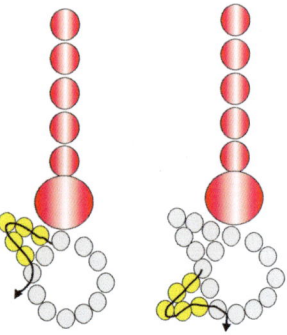

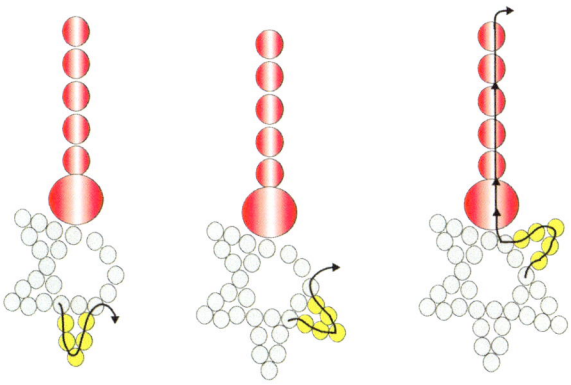

3. Stitch up into the fringe strand and pull the thread to adjust the tension.

Leaf End

This end is typically done with 11/0 beads but 15/0 beads can be used. In the example that follows, the leaf is designed with four beads on the leaf sides but other counts (more and less) can be used

1. Pick up the beads for the fringe strand plus seven seed beads. Skip the last bead and stitch back through the bead above it. Hold and pull the last bead with one hand and pull the thread with the other hand to adjust the tension.

2. Pick up 4 seed beads and stitch up through the first seed bead and up the fringe strand. Hold and pull the bottom bead with one hand and pull the thread with the other hand to adjust the tension again as needed.

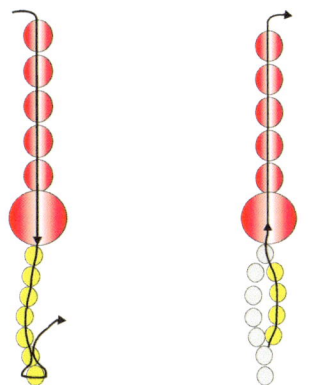

Loop End

This technique can be used with any type of bead and is the best method for including a top drilled bead at the end of fringe. There are two different thread paths shown in the options below. The size of the beads used to create the loops must be larger than the hole in the bead above.

Steps Option 1: (when end beads are small, light or when using doubled thread).

1. Pick up the beads for the fringe strand.

2. Decide how many beads to use for each side of the loop. Pick up those beads, the bottom bead and beads for the other side, then stitch back up the fringe strand.

3. Hold and pull the bottom bead with one hand and pull on the thread with the other hand to adjust the tension. Release the bottom bead and pull the thread with the other hand for a final adjustment.

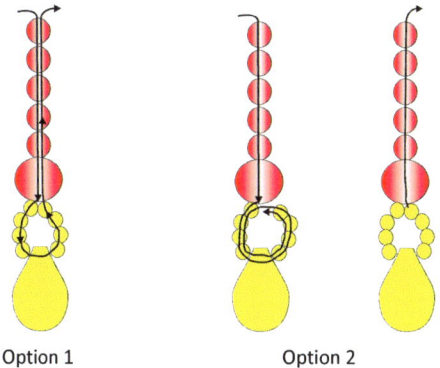

Option 1   Option 2

Steps Option 2: (when end beads are large, heavy and using single thread)

1. Pick up the beads for the fringe strand.

2. Decide how many beads to use for each side of the loop. Pick up those beads, the bottom bead and beads for the other side.

3. Stitch through the loop beads (each side and bottom bead) again to create a loop. Pull to adjust the tension. Stitch back up the fringe strand and pull again to adjust the tension.

Attaching fringe to beadwork

Fringe is a great way to add pizazz to the design of beadwork. The objective is to stitch the fringe into the edge in a way that compliments and enhances the beadwork already done. Fringe can be heavy and the movement of fringe will create a pull on the beadwork beyond its' true weight due to the centrifugal force created by movement. Therefore, the main consideration is to spread the stress when attaching to beadwork so as not to create a seam or pull the beadwork in a way that negatively impacts the design in the beadwork. The illustrations that follow show suggested stitch paths to use to attach fringe to popular types of beadwork.

The main principles are:

- Attach fringe directly into a bead hole where possible (figure 1).

- Attach fringe between beads (figure 2) versus around a bead (figure 3) when the edge of the beadwork does not provide a bead hole. While it is possible to attach fringe around a bead, it is extremely difficult to obtain proper tension and not have a gap between the beadwork and the fringe top. You need to pull very tight to eliminate the gap. But pulling tight on thread makes a straight line while going around a bead means the thread has to turn corners. These conflicting forces make getting a proper tension correct very difficult. See tip at right.

- Vary the levels up into the beadwork to secure fringe so as not to produce a seam from the pull of the weight of the fringe.

Tip: If you must attach around a bead, first pull to a tight tension on one side of the bead. Then stitch into the other side of the bead and pull the fringe to the center as illustrated in figures 4 and 5.

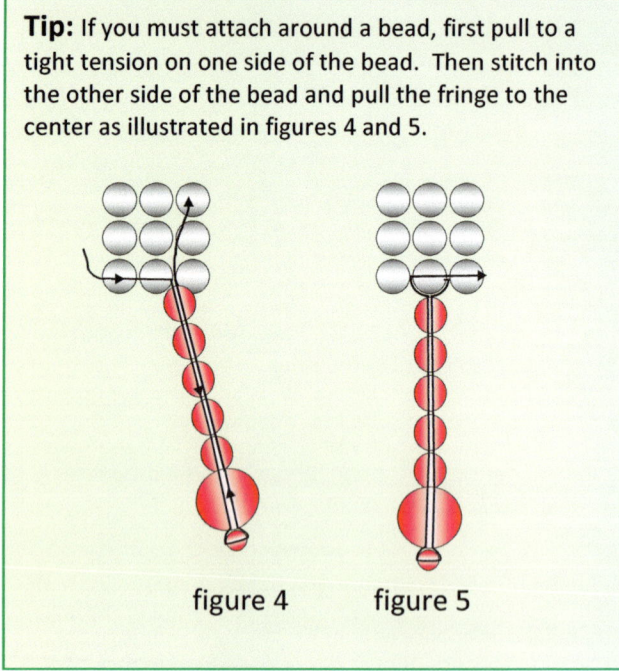

figure 4   figure 5

Loom/square stitch - hole edge

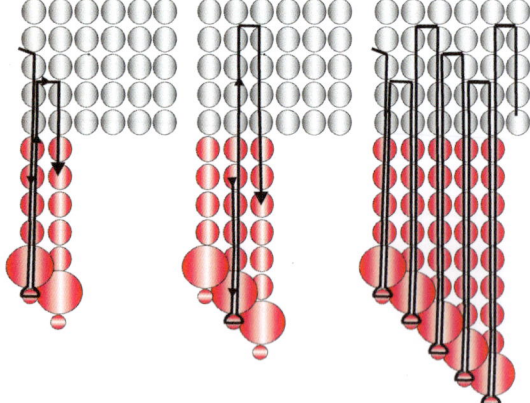

Loom/square stitch – side of bead edge

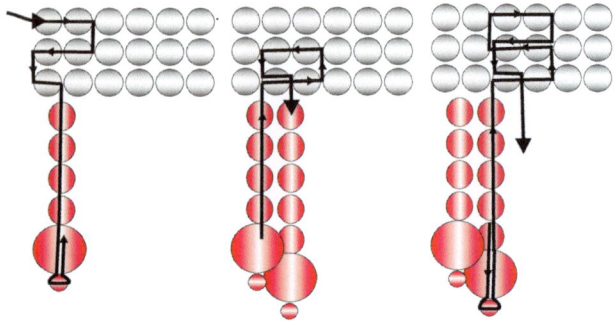

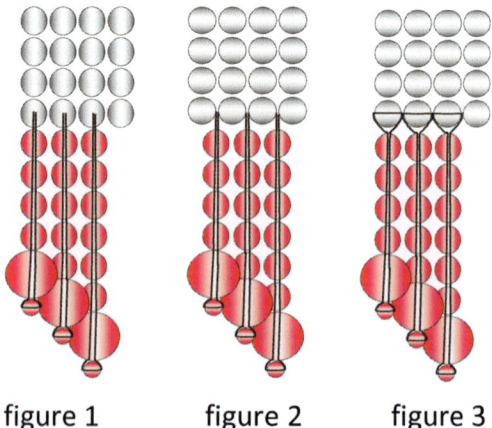

figure 1   figure 2   figure 3

- Follow the stitch path of the beadwork to secure the fringe stitching into the bead holes, not across or over beads.

12

Peyote and Brick Stitch – hole edge

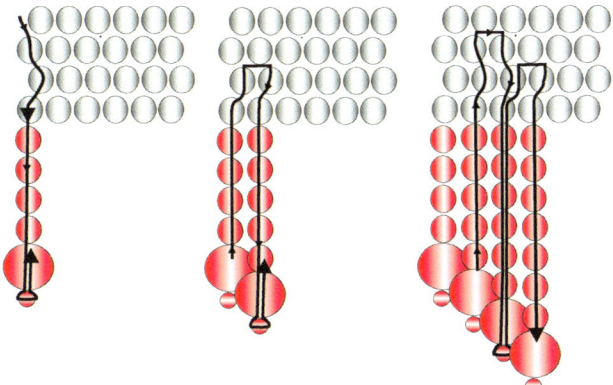

Herringbone - side of bead edge

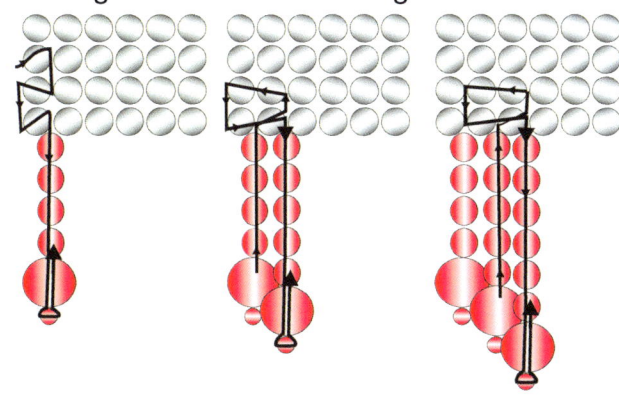

Peyote and Brick Stitch - side of bead edge

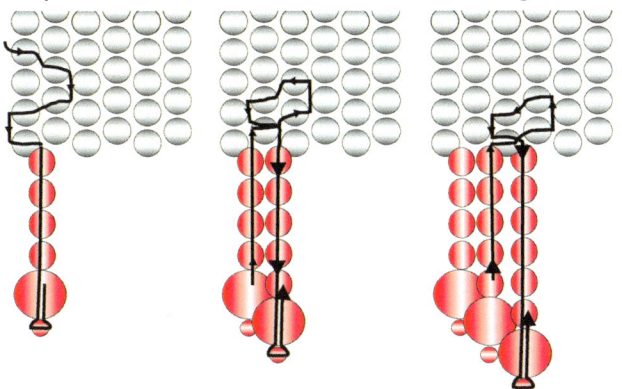

Right angle Weave

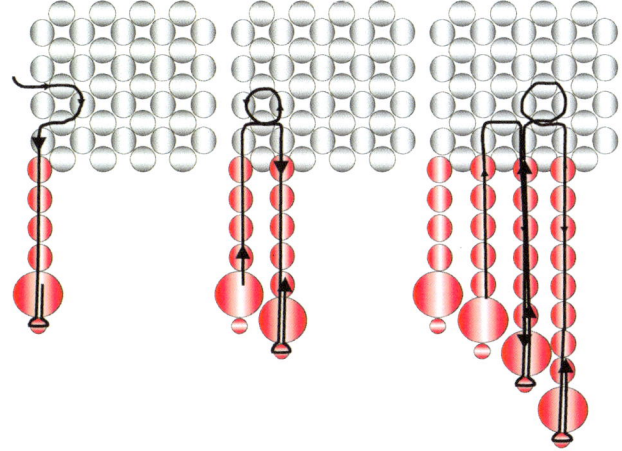

Herringbone – hole edge

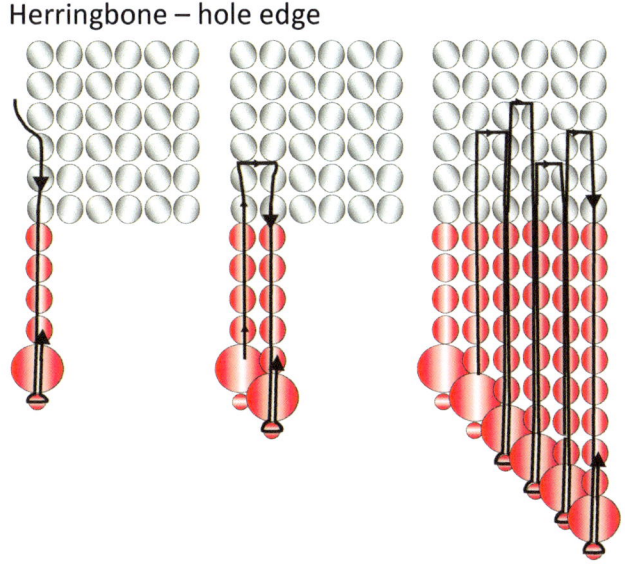

Bead embroidered edge (Sunshine edge aka basic edge, raw edge, brick stitch edge)

Anchor the fringe by stitching through the backings. Do not simply hook through the edge beads.

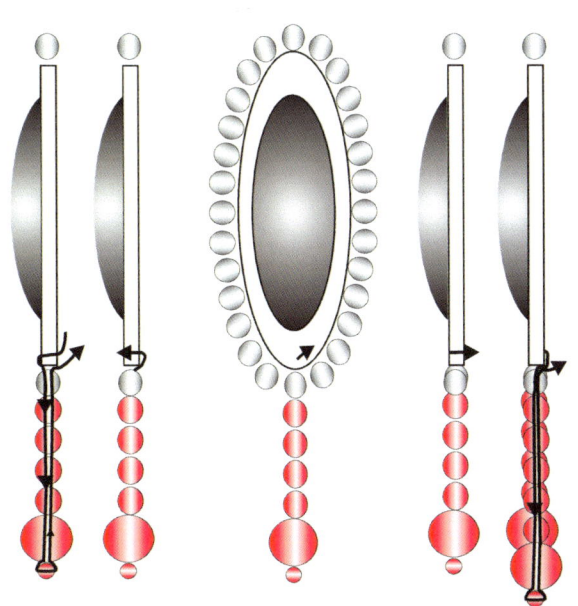

Designing fringe:

Fringe is a fabulous design element to add to your creations. There are many different techniques and each is described in the next sections including considerations for designing each type. No matter what type of fringe you choose to include in your design, there are two fundamentals that should be considered. These relate to the two errors most commonly seen in fringe design.

Proportion

Fringe is typically just one element in the design of a beaded piece which has many other design elements. In the best designs, the fringe fits with the entire piece to form a coherent whole. When you see that piece, the fringe is an integral part of the design and you can't imagine the piece without the fringe. Each part of the fringe including:

- the type of fringe
- the number of fringe strands
- the length of the fringe strands
- the colors of the beads used
- the size of the beads in the fringe

all co-ordinate and compliment the piece as a whole as exemplified in Photos 1 and 2.

If a piece of beadwork is large or chunky or wild, a few short fringe strands will be out of proportion and will look like the designer thought about fringe but there was no commitment to add it to the design, like in Photo 3. This fringe is out of proportion to the other elements in the design. There are too few strands and they are too short and too simple in design as compared to the piece as a whole. Likewise, a small delicate demure piece with large beads and too many fringe strands will overwhelm the design and might diminish the success of the design as a whole. Think of the fringe as an integral element of the beadwork, not just something you are adding on. Look at the beadwork already done for clues to decide the fringe type, number of strands, length, etc.

Table fringe

This is a term used to describe fringe that looks great when lying on a table, but has a very different (and not attractive) appearance when worn. When beadwork is displayed and photographed lying on a table, the fringe can be spread out so that each fringe is shown and gravity has no impact on the design. If your creation is for a contest or a show where you only need to photograph it lying down, your design alternatives are infinite. However, if you are designing and creating a piece that will be worn, then gravity and body shape need to be considered. The best and easiest way to avoid creating table fringe is to lift up your beadwork often as you are creating your fringe. Lift and hold it up as it will be oriented on the body and evaluate the effect of gravity on the appearance of the fringe. While there are no rules, there are consequences for design choices. The projects and design discussions concentrate on the perspective of wearing a piece rather than "table fringe".

Photo 1   Photo 2   Photo 3

Chapter 3: Standard Fringe

As a general rule, standard fringe is created with single thread. You stitch down through the fringe strand and then back up resulting in doubled thread in the fringe strand. Using doubled thread (resulting in four thread strands in the fringe) is recommended if your beads are particularly heavy, you desire a stiffer fringe strand, or just want the beads to line up straighter.

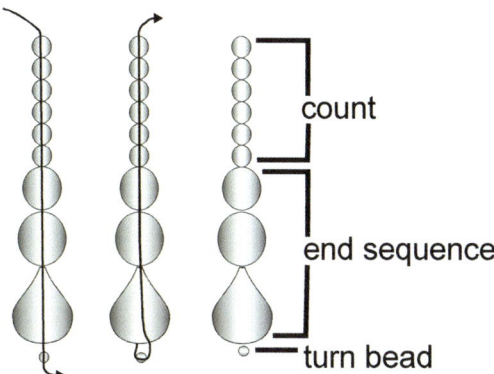

Steps: (Using a standard turn bead end)

1. Exit the beadwork where you want to attach the fringe.

2. Pick up beads for the strand plus a turn bead. Move the beads all the way up thread to sit next to the beadwork.

3. Stitch back through the beads in step 2, skipping the turn bead and stitch up into the beadwork.

4. Hold the turn bead with one hand and pull down while using the other hand to pull the thread up. This ensures that the two threads in the strand are both straight and have equal tension. First, pull to achieve the perfect tension. Then pull just a little tighter. The more seed beads in the strand, the more tension to add beyond the perfect tension.

Tip: Note that you stitch into the beadwork before adjusting the tension. If you adjust the tension and then stitch into the beadwork, the action of stitching into the beadwork will impact the tension in the strand and you'll have to adjust it all over again.

Tip: Beads are not perfectly shaped, even after culling. Just as water seeks its own level, beads will twist and rotate in the strand until they position themselves with the least amount of stress. If you leave the strand at the perfect tension, you will shortly end up with a gap as the beads settle and move. This movement is the cause of the gap, not the thread being stretched, which is sometimes blamed.

Troubleshooting:

Fringe that is too stiff –
This can be caused by a variety of factors. One possibility is that the thread is too thick or stiff. Solve this by using Nymo or Silamide, or similar product in "A" or "B" weight. Do not use Fireline, Power Pro or similar poly thread products since these are stiffer threads.

Too much tension (pulling too much on the thread) can also cause stiff fringe. Some beaders are prone to tight beading. In this case, curl the fringe around your finger in a "U" shape to introduce some ease into the strand before proceeding to the next fringe.

Fringe that is too loose (gaps show)-
Try using doubled thread to fill the bead holes more completely and make the beads line up better with each other. This is a good solution for cylinder beads (like Delicas or Tohos) or other beads with a large hole; filling the hole forces the beads to line up straight and not tilt. The strand may end up less flexible, but will look better than if gaps are showing.

Fringe has two threads, one stitched down and around the turn bead and the other back up. Make sure each side of the thread is pulled to the proper length. If the sides are uneven, then over time, the beads will move creating a gap. Pull on the turn bead to straighten and adjust the first side of the thread as you pull the needle thread to adjust the other side of the thread.

Always pull the tension in fringe just a little tighter than you consider perfect, bendable flowing fringe. Beads are not shaped perfectly and they will twist and turn to fit more easily with each other which will create a shorter length of beads and therefore a gap. The thread did not stretch or grow, the beads settled into each other. Pull the tension slightly tighter than needed for a perfect tension when you create the fringe so that over time as the beads move, the tension will ease for a bendable fringe. If there are more beads (particularly seed beads) add more tension; for short strands add very little extra tension.

How to design standard fringe:

In the simplest situation, standard fringe is a count of seed beads followed by an end sequence of other beads.

- Select the beads, both seeds and others you may want to use in the fringe.

- Thread a needle with a 1/2 yard of thread and put on a stop bead. Use this to design your end sequence, selecting beads and changing the order until you have a design you like. As a general rule, the largest bead is at the bottom of the end sequence but this is not required.

- Start in the center of the area to be fringed. Pick up seed beads until you have the length desired. Set the end sequence created above at the bottom to determine the total length for the fringe. Adjust as desired adding or removing seed beads until you have the final count for the seed bead section to achieve the total fringe length desired. Write that number down.

- Determine your decrease/increase. The increase/decrease is the change in the count of seed beads before adding the end sequence and is a function of two design choices, both relating to the final appearance of the fringe.

One is the bottom shape of the fringe, as shown in the photos on page 17. For a straight bottom, there is no increase or decrease. For a "V" shape, decrease the count of subsequent fringes by 1 or more, the larger the decrease number, the deeper the "V". For a "U" shape, create the center fringe and at least one on each side of it using the same count. Then decrease for the remaining fringes. You can also create with a "W" shape like the project on page 22 by decreasing, then increasing, then decreasing again. For a "\" shape, increase for fringes to one side and decrease for fringes to the other side. You can use your imagination to create many profiles for the end using these increase and decrease techniques.

The other design choice relates to the size of the beads in the end sequence and how you want the fringe to lay. If the end sequence has a bead that is 5mm or larger AND you want the fringe to lay relatively flat when worn, then the decrease needs to be at least 3. If you chose a chunky appearance where the fringes will hang over each other, any decrease can be used.

Straight Bottom    "V" Shape    "U" Shape

"W" Shape    " / " Shape

- Use the decrease and count determined in the previous steps to plan all the subsequent fringes to one side. Do this by writing down the count for each subsequent fringe. You can use a needle and thread to create the final fringe on one side which will help you envision the entire fringe section. This will also show you if there are enough seed beads in the count to perform all the decreases. Adjust as needed or desired including changing the count or changing the end sequence. If the count goes to zero before the last fringes, you can eliminate beads in the end sequence, replacing with seed beads to add to the count. For example, in the necklace (photo right) the center fringe has a count of 34 plus an end sequence and used a decrease of 3. While creating from the center to the right, at column 28 there were no more count beads so the end sequence was adjusted. To accomplish this, first re-create the previous fringe eliminating beads as needed in the end sequence and replacing with as many seed beads as are needed to span the distance of the removed end sequence beads. Use this new definition (new count and new end sequence) and continue to create fringes with the standard defined decrease.

Original End Sequence:

Bulge bead	
11/0 grey	
4mm bicone	
11/0 grey	
Bugle bead	
(3 ea.) 11/0 grey	
(3 ea.) 11/0 pink	
3mm bicone	
4mm round pink	
4mm round silver	
6mm round	
11/0 grey turn bead	

In this necklace, each fringe is the same design with only a change in the count beads. However, this is not required and in the case of large end beads is often not recommended.

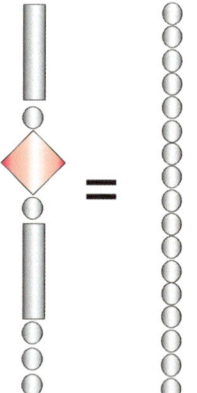   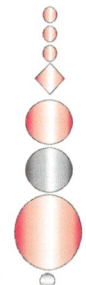

Replace with seeds   New End Sequence

- The typical situation is for each fringe to be the same design.

This necklace includes a 10mm Swarovski marguerite bead at the end of the fringe attached with a loop end. This is included only every third fringe to provide adequate space between the ends so that each marguerite bead is visible. If each end included the marguerite bead, then they would overlap each other and you would only see a band of orange instead of the profile of the bead. Often large end components are heavy and expensive. Spacing the usage of these components to every other, every third, fourth, etc. fringe end will control the total weight of the beadwork and highlights the unique and special nature of the components since each is visible. See Project 3 on page 24 and the variation on page 24 for some examples and see the photos below.

left. Work with two needles and thread and do one or two strands to the right and then switch to the other needle on the left to execute one or two fringes there. This is different from the standard approach of creating the center fringe, then all fringes to the right and finishing with all fringes to the left.

- Fringe can be the same design or alternating designs or, as in the photos that follow, each fringe can have its own unique design. This design type is "Confetti Fringe". The execution of this type of design is both easier and more difficult than other fringe design styles. The best way to execute this is to start in the center like typical fringe. Then create the strand on the right and then the strand on the

- Designing fringe can include shading of colors down the length of the fringe (see page 27), shading of colors across the width of the fringe (page 28), and using alternate end sequences (page 24). The design of the fringe can change within the fringe (page 20) or even create a picture (page 30). Use seed and other beads to open your imagination.

Projects:

The necklace projects that follow use similar basic techniques to create the base and the necklace strands. This allows for more project examples and provides a format where you can concentrate on the fringe techniques and the design lessons and alternatives within each project. There are also a variety of embellishing techniques. You can easily do a mix and match of the fringing and embellishing to create your own unique necklace design. There is nothing like experience to really learn a technique, so creating the necklaces will give you an intensive, repetitious "workshop" to learn the fringe techniques. However, if you want a quicker experience, you can use the earring projects on page 32. Create these earring projects as photographed or substitute with the colors and fringe designs in the necklace projects using the same base construction method from the earring project.

Project 1 – Standard Fringe:

This project uses the picot end (page 10) and introduces the concept of a decrease within the end sequence as a part of the design.

Supplies:

5 grams seed beads 11/0 green color lined
3 grams seed beads 11/0 royal blue luster
2 grams seed beads 11/0 metallic gold
1 gram seed beads 15/0 metallic gold
1 gram seed beads 6/0 blue
31 each teardrop beads faceted 8x6mm sapphire AB
31 each round beads 4mm transparent blue
47 each bicone beads Swarovski 4mm fern green
62 each bicone beads Swarovski 3mm fern green
15 each flat rectangle beads 8x12mm transparent sapphire
Standard beading kit (page 92)
Standard necklace kit (page 92) gold

Steps:

1. Create a ladder with 31 columns of two green 11/0 seed beads using the instructions for Basic 2-bead Ladder Stitch on page 88.

2. Cut 6 yards of thread and put on a stop bead with a 3 yard tail to use the Half-thread Method (page 87).

3. Start in the center, stitching down into the 16th column (center) and create the center fringe and all fringes to the right. Then use the tail thread to create the fringes to the left. Pick up one seed bead at the top of the column, after creating the fringe for that column and stitch down to the next column for the next fringe. Use the chart below for the seed bead count using the 11/0 green beads plus the end sequence. Note that the decrease is a total of three, with 2 in the top count and 1 within the end sequence. Knot the thread, weave in and cut.

Fringe Chart:

Column	count	end sequence count
center	30	15
15, 17	28	14
14, 18	26	13
13, 19	24	12
12, 20	22	11
11, 21	20	10
10, 22	18	9
9, 23	16	8
8, 24	14	7
7, 25	12	6
6, 26	10	5
5, 27	8	4
4, 28	6	3
3, 29	4	2
2, 30	2	1
1, 31	0	0

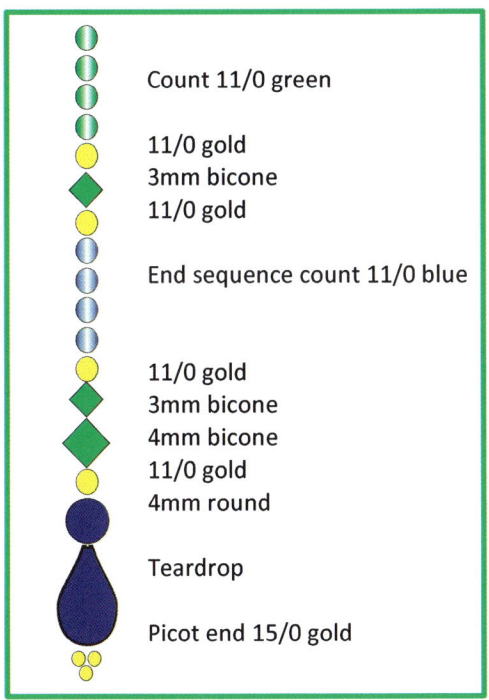

Count 11/0 green

11/0 gold
3mm bicone
11/0 gold

End sequence count 11/0 blue

11/0 gold
3mm bicone
4mm bicone
11/0 gold
4mm round

Teardrop

Picot end 15/0 gold

4. Cut one yard of thread and put a needle on to work single thread. Add a stop bead with a 9 inch tail.

5. Stitch down through the top bead of the ladder column three over from the center to the right. Pick up one rectangle bead and stitch up through the top bead of the ladder column three over from the center to the left. Stitch down through the next column and up through the bottom bead of the previous column. Stitch through the rectangle bead again and down through the bottom bead of the ladder column on the right. Stitch up through the next column and down through the top bead of the previous ladder column and through the rectangle bead again.

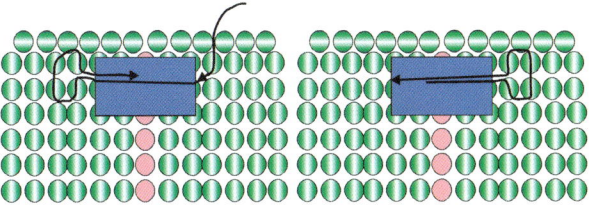

6. Pick up one 4mm bicone and three 15/0 beads. Stitch back through the bicone and rectangle treating the three 15/0 beads like a Picot End (page 10). Repeat on the right side. Stitch through the ladder column underneath. Knot the threads, weave in and cut.

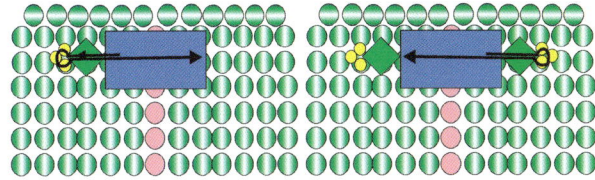

7. Use the illustration below with the rectangle, 4mm bicone and 11/0 gold beads and instructions for Necklace Strand with Side Attachment on page 89 and create the necklace strands.

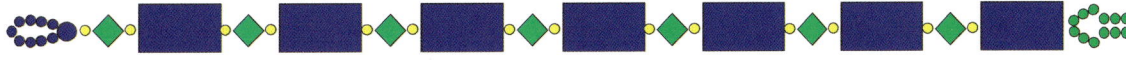

Project 2 – Standard Fringe:

This project uses the star end (page 10) and introduces a new profile for the end of the fringe of a "W" shape. Before beginning the project read the discussion on page 24 of an alternate design choice concerning alternating end sequences.

Supplies:

7 grams seed beads 11/0 purple shimmer
4 grams seed beads 11/0 dark green rainbow
2 grams seed beads 11/0 gold metallic
6 grams seed beads 15/0 gold metallic
2 grams bugle beads 6mm gold metallic
1 gram 6/0 purple transparent
109 each Czech fire polish beads 4mm dark purple metallic
16 each Puffed diamond beads 12x8mm green/purple iris
3 each star beads 8mm gold metallic
1 each star beads 6mm gold metallic
Standard beading kit (page 92)
Standard necklace kit (page 92) gold

Steps:

1. Create a ladder with 31 columns of two purple 11/0 seed beads using the instructions for Basic 2-bead Ladder Stitch on page 88.

ooooooooooooooooooooooooooooooo
ooooooooooooooooooooooooooooooo

2. Cut 6 yards of thread and put on a stop bead with a 3 yard tail to use the Half-thread Method (page 87).

3. Start in the center, stitching down into the 16th column (center). Create the center fringe and all fringes to the right. Then use the tail thread for the fringes to the left. Pick up one seed bead at the top of the column, after creating the fringe for that column and stitch down to the next column for the next fringe. Use the chart below for the seed bead count using the 11/0 purple beads plus the end sequence. Note that the count is a decrease of 3, then increases by 3 and finally decreases again by 3. Knot the thread, weave in the ends and cut.

Fringe Chart:

Column	count
center	30
15, 17	27
14, 18	24
13, 19	21
12, 20	18
11, 21	15
10, 22	12
9, 23	15
8, 24	18
7, 25	21
6, 26	18
5, 27	15
4, 28	12
3, 29	9
2, 30	6
1, 31	3

End Sequence:

Bugle bead

10 each 11/0 green

4mm purple
11/0 gold
4mm purple
11/0 gold
4mm purple
11/0 purple
Star End with 15/0 gold

15/0 (turn bead). Stitch back through the star. Hold the turn bead with one hand and pull the thread with the other hand to adjust the tension. Pick up fifteen gold 15/0 beads and stitch through the top bead 8th from the end. Stitch down into the ladder below.

6. Stitch up the next column and through the top bead above. Repeat step 5 except pick up sixteen 15/0 beads, one 6mm star, one 15/0, one 8mm star and one 15/0 bead (turn bead) and stitch over into the top bead 11th from the other side.

7. Stitch up the next column and through the top bead above. Repeat step 5.

8. Knot the thread ends, weave in and cut.

9. Use the illustration below with the diamond, 4mm fire polish and 11/0 gold beads and instructions for Necklace Strand with Side Attachment page 89 and create the necklace strand.

4. Put a needle on 1 yard of thread and move it to the middle to work doubled thread. Add a stop bead with a nine inch tail. Stitch up though the 2 beads in the ladder in the second column from the end and through the bead above.

5. Pick up fifteen gold 15/0 beads, one 8mm star and one

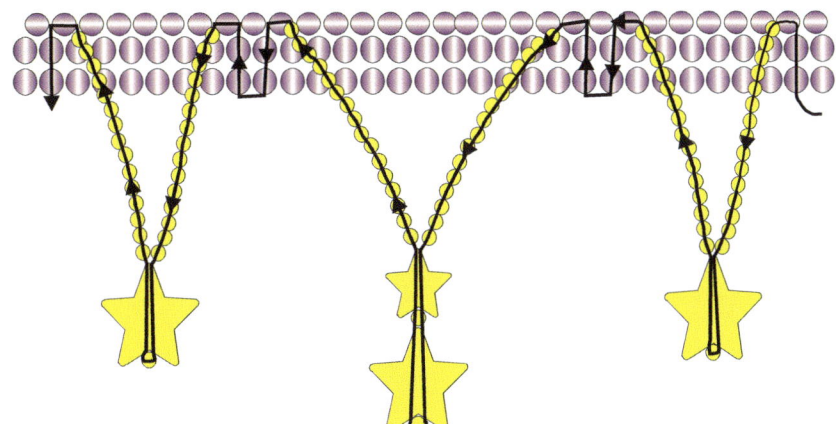

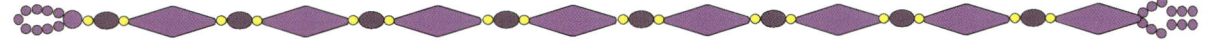

Alternate Version – alternating the end bead technique

This necklace is just like Project 2 except that the star ends are included only on every other fringe strand alternating with a Standard Turn Bead. Since the star is large, the fringe is thicker when a star end is on each strand as in the project version. Alternating a star end on every other strand makes the individual stars more visible. Since there is more room between the stars, a decrease of two was used instead of three. Both methods will work, but there is a difference of appearance and time to execute. This example is included to help you understand the effect of a design choice to include on each end or on only some of the end sequences.

Project 3 – Standard Fringe

Both the Loop end Option 2 (page 11) and the standard turn bead are used in this project. This necklace is an example of using an alternate end sequence designed to highlight the large bead on the end loops. Alternating the end sequences allows large end beads to be seen more clearly and is often needed to manage the weight of a beaded creation so that it is comfortable to wear since it is not as heavy as it would be if the large bead was used on each fringe.

24

Supplies:

5 grams seed beads 11/0 blue color lined lime
2 grams seed beads 11/0 opaque light green matte
2 grams bugle beads twisted 6mm lime rainbow
1 gram seed beads 6/0 teal
94 each round bead 4mm teal
92 each round bead 6mm teal
14 each Leaf drop 15 x 22mm teal
1 each flower bead center drilled 20mm lime
2 each connector 2 strand gold
Standard beading kit (page 92)
Standard necklace kit (page 92) gold

Steps:

1. Create a ladder with 31 columns of two lime 11/0 seed beads using the instructions for Basic 2-bead Ladder Stitch on page 88.

2. Cut 6 yards of thread and put on a stop bead with a 3 yard tail to use the Half-thread Method (page 87). Start in the center, stitching down into the 16th column (center). Create the center fringe and all fringes to the right. Then use the tail and create the fringes to the left. Use the chart below for the count seed beads using the 11/0 lime beads plus the end sequences. Knot the thread, weave in and cut.

End Sequence A

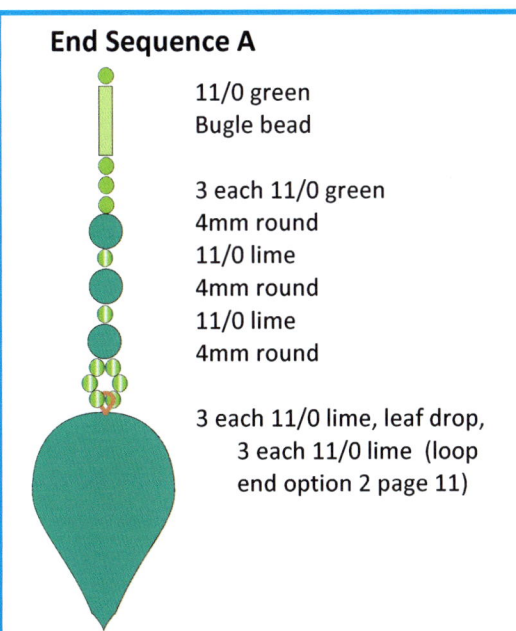

11/0 green
Bugle bead

3 each 11/0 green
4mm round
11/0 lime
4mm round
11/0 lime
4mm round

3 each 11/0 lime, leaf drop, 3 each 11/0 lime (loop end option 2 page 11)

End Sequence B

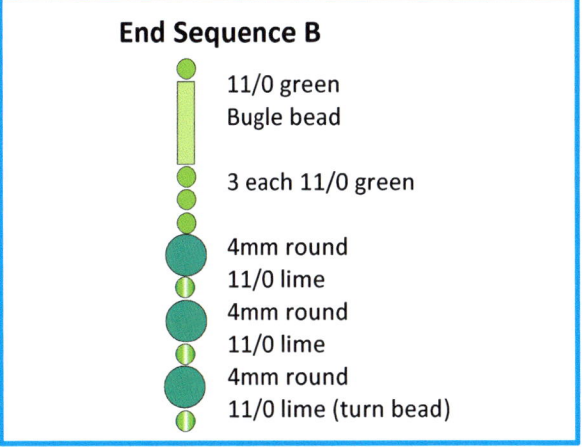

11/0 green
Bugle bead

3 each 11/0 green

4mm round
11/0 lime
4mm round
11/0 lime
4mm round
11/0 lime (turn bead)

Fringe Chart:

Column	count	End Sequence
center	31	A
15, 17	29	B
14, 18	27	B
13, 19	25	A
12, 20	23	B
11, 21	21	B
10, 22	19	A
9, 23	17	B
8, 24	15	B
7, 25	13	A
6, 26	11	B
5, 27	9	B
4, 28	7	A
3, 29	5	B
2, 30	3	B
1, 31	1	A

Tip: When alternating the end sequences, first decide which end sequence to use on the center and on the last fringes on each side. Then select a spacing that creates the look you want (alternate every other one, or every third as in this project, etc.) and plan out how that will work on a chart. Typically, the design will include the large end sequence (like End Sequence A in the project) as the center fringe and the last fringes on the side. In the case of this project the spacing works out perfectly. If you need to adjust the pattern to end with a large bead, put the adjustments either in the center area or at the far sides depending on the appearance you would like to achieve.

3. Use figure 6 below with the 6mm rounds 11/0 lime beads and instructions for Necklace Strand with Side Attachment on page 89 and create the necklace strand.

4. Cut 1 yard of thread and put on a needle to work single thread. Pick up one 6/0 bead, one flower, one 4mm round and one 11/0 lime and move to leave a 9 inch tail. Stitch back through the 4mm and flower and enter the 6/0 bead on the other side. Stitch to the front again through the flower, 4mm and 11/0, back again through the 4mm and flower and through the 6/0 bead to reinforce.

5. Pick up four 11/0 lime beads and stitch around the 6/0 bead and through the first 11/0 bead. (figure 1) Create a fringe using nine 11/0 lime and a bottom loop using three 11/0 lime, a leaf, and three 11/0 lime. Stitch up into the top loop and through one more bead. (figure 2)

6. Create another fringe using eleven 11/0 lime and a bottom loop using three 11/0 lime, a leaf, and three 11/0 lime. Stitch up into the top loop and through one more bead. (figure 3)

7. Create another fringe using six 11/0 lime and a bottom loop using three 11/0 lime, a leaf, and three 11/0 lime. Stitch around the loop one more time to reinforce. Knot the thread ends, weave in and cut. (figure 4)

8. Cut 3 yards of thread and put a needle on. Move the needle to the center to work doubled thread. Use figure 7 below with the 6mm round and 11/0 lime beads and instructions for Stringing with Thread on page 89 and create the necklace strand.

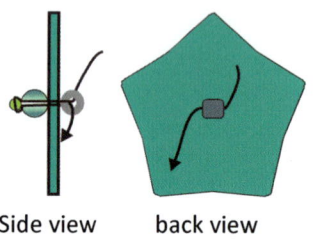

Side view   back view

Tip: Use steps 5 to 8 to create fringe excitement on shank-type buttons and step 9 to string it into a fabulous necklace.

figure 1   figure 2   figure 3   figure 4   figure 5

figure 6

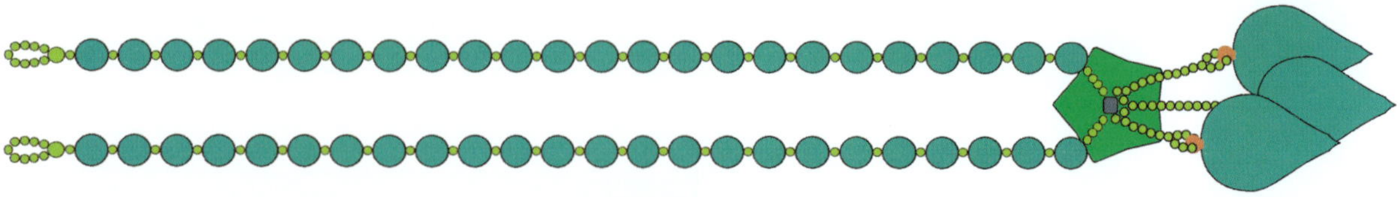

figure 7

Project 4 – Standard Fringe:

A standard turn bead is used in this project which is an example of how to shade colors down the fringe design. One way of shading is to choose a color and then select beads that are varying shades (from light to dark) of the same color. Another way is to use completely different colors as in the project. One key to using different colors is to use the same finish for all or most of the colors. In the project below the beads have an AB finish except for the orange which has a shimmer from the crackle. This provides a similarity and continuity so it blends the different colors. The colors used are the same deep intensity and this also creates a blending that works. For instance, this project done in pastel shades of all ceylon or pearl finishes would also be wonderful.

This project is also an example of using large beads inside the fringe design providing a full and chunky fringe. Note also the variation of technique used on the side fringes to flatten the profile.

Supplies:
5 grams seed beads 11/0 cobalt opaque rainbow
1 gram seed beads 11/0 amber transparent rainbow
1 gram seed beads 11/0 red transparent rainbow
2 grams seed beads Delicas 8/0 cobalt opaque rainbow
87 each beads round 3mm dark green transparent rainbow
87 each beads rondelle 5mm amber transparent rainbow
29 each beads round crackle 6mm orange
29 each beads oval 4x6mm red transparent rainbow
29 each beads round 6mm red transparent rainbow
2 each bead round 3mm dark blue transparent
1 each bead striped foil oval 25x30mm cobalt
20 each bead oval 8x10mm cobalt opaque rainbow
Standard beading kit (page 92)
Standard necklace kit (page 92) gold

Steps:
1. Create a ladder with 33 columns of blue 8/0 seed beads using the instructions for Basic 1-bead Ladder Stitch on page 88.

2. Cut 6 yards of thread and put on a stop bead with a 3 yard tail to use the Half-thread Method (page 87). Start in the center, stitching down into the 17th column (center) Create that fringe and fringes to the right. Use the tail thread for left fringes. Use the chart below for the seed bead count using the 11/0 beads for the count plus the end sequence. On columns 1 and 2, 3 and 4, 30 and 31, 32 and 33, split the count to attach to two beads on the ladder as in Sequence B. This will thin the chunky aspect of the fringe on each side.

Tip: When splitting the count and using two connection points to attach to the beadwork (as in sequence B), use only the top two or three beads of the count as the area to split. Using only a few beads above the split point provides for easier, better tension control.

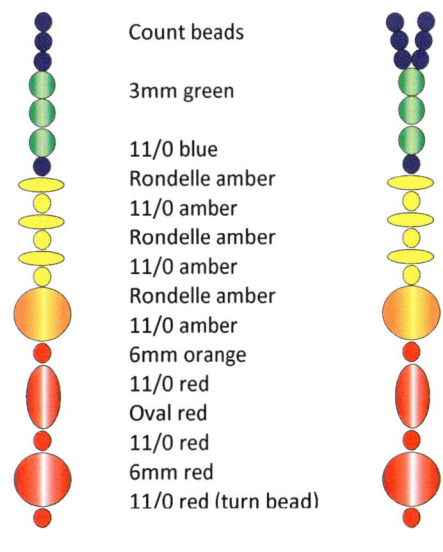

Count beads
3mm green
11/0 blue
Rondelle amber
11/0 amber
Rondelle amber
11/0 amber
Rondelle amber
11/0 amber
6mm orange
11/0 red
Oval red
11/0 red
6mm red
11/0 red (turn bead)

Sequence A   Sequence B

Fringe Chart:

Column	count	Style
center	10	A
16, 18	10	A
15, 19	10	A
14, 20	10	A
13, 21	10	A
12, 22	9	A
11, 23	8	A
10, 24	7	A
9, 25	6	A
8, 26	5	A
7, 27	4	A
6, 28	3	A
5, 29	3	A
4, 30	3	B
Repeat on remaining		

Project 5 - Standard Fringe:

This project uses a standard turn bead and introduces a method to shade and blend colors across fringe strands. Similar to blending down a fringe strand (see page 27), the beads have the same/similar finishes and intensities of color which assist in the visual appeal of the blending.

3. Use the illustration below with the 8x10mm oval and 11/0 blue beads and instructions for Necklace Strand with Side Attachment on page 89 and create the necklace strand.

4. Cut 1 yard of thread and put a needle on to work single thread. Add a stop bead with a 9 inch tail. Stitch up through the eighth bead from one side of the ladder. Pick up one 4mm blue, the large blue oval and one 4mm blue bead. Stitch down through the eighth bead from the other end and up through the ninth bead and stitch through the added beads again. Stitch down through the 9th bead. Repeat the thread path twice more to reinforce. Remove the stop bead, tie a knot, weave in and cut the threads.

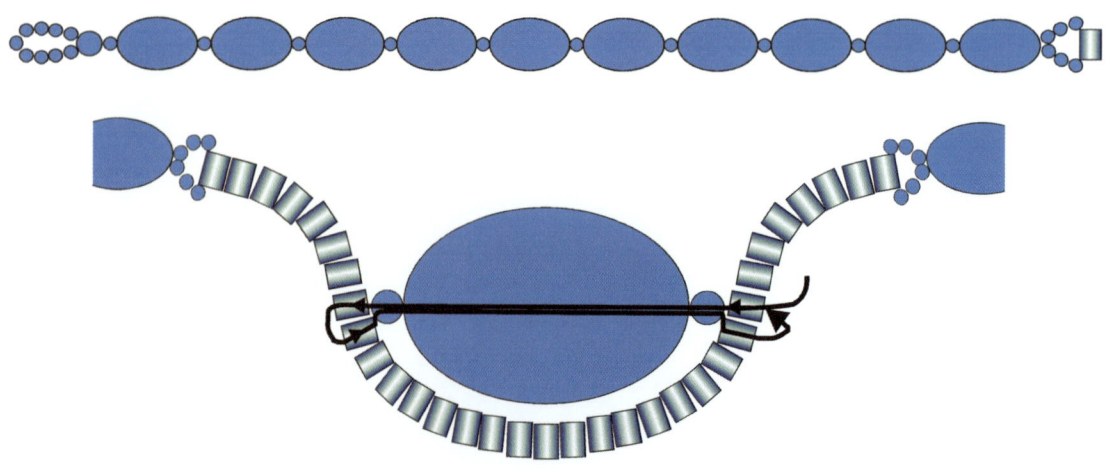

Supplies:

4 grams seed beads 11/0 lavender color lined (color A)
4 grams seed beads 11/0 turquoise color lined (color B)
3 grams seed beads 11/0 light olive color lined (color C)
3 grams seed beads 11/0 pink color lined (color D)
2 grams seed beads 11/0 silver metallic
1 gram seed beads 6/0 lavender metallic AB
14 each beads bicone 3mm provence lavender AB 2X (color A)
12 each beads bicone 4mm provence lavender AB 2X (color A)
12 each beads round pearl 4mm lavender (color A)
16 each beads bicone 3mm aqua AB 2X (color B)
24 each beads bicone 4mm turquoise AB 2X (color B)
20 each beads round pearl 4mm aqua (color B)
21 each beads bicone 3mm erinite color B (color C)
36 each beads bicone 4mm fern green AB 2X (color C)
16 each beads round pearl 4mm olive green (color C)
12 each beads bicone 3mm rose (color D)
8 each beads bicone 4mm Indian pink AB 2X (color D)
14 each beads round pearl 4mm pink (color D)
29 each beads round pearl 6mm lavender
6 each beads bicone 6mm turquoise AB 2X
1 each pendant triangle dichroic glass 12x20mm
24 each beads bicone 4mm turquoise AB 2X
20 each beads round pearl 4mm aqua
Standard beading kit (page 92)
Standard necklace kit (page 92) silver

Steps:

1. Create a ladder with 31 columns using the instructions for Basic 2-bead Ladder Stitch on page 88. Create the first 3 columns in pink, the next 4 with olive, the next 5 with turquoise. Use lavender for the center 7 and finish with the other colors used previously in reverse order (end with pink).

2. Cut 6 yards of thread and put on a stop bead with a 3 yard tail to use the Half-thread Method (page 87). Start in the center, stitching down into the 16th column (center). Create that fringe and fringes to the right. Use the tail thread for left fringes. Pick up one seed bead at the top of the column, after creating the fringe for that column and stitch down to the next column for the next fringe. See the chart below for the count and bead colors to use. Knot the thread, weave in the ends and cut.

End Sequence: Use (color) as specified in the fringe chart

 3mm bicone (color)
3mm bicone (color)
Silver 11/0
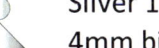 4mm bicone (color)
4mm bicone (color)
Silver 11/0
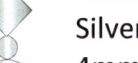 4mm round pearl (color)
Silver 11/0
4mm round pearl (color)
 Silver 11/0 (turn bead)

Fringe Chart:

Colum	count and color	end sequence colors
Center	35 - A	AA AA A A
15,17	33 - A	AA AA A A
14,18	31 – pattern AAB	AA AA A A
13,19	29 – pattern AB	AA BB A B
12,20	27 – pattern ABB	BB BB B B
11,21	25 – B	BB BB B B
10,22	23 – B	BB BB B B
9,23	21 – pattern BBC	BB BB B B
8,24	19 – pattern BC	BB CC B C
7,25	17 – pattern BCC	CC CC C C
6,26	15 – C	CC CC C C
5,27	13 – C	CC CC C C
4,28	11 – pattern CCD	CC CC D C
3,29	9 – pattern CDD	DD CC D D
2,30	7 - D	DD DD D D
1,31	5 - D	DD DD D D

3. Use figure 1 (next page) with the 6mm pearls, silver and lavender 11/0 beads, the 6mm bicones and the 4mm fern green bicones with the instructions for Necklace Strand with Side Attachment on page 89 and create the necklace strand.

4. Cut 1 yard of thread and put a needle on to work single thread. Add a stop bead with a 9 inch tail.

5. Stitch down through the beads in the 4th column and up one bead into the 5th column. Pick up one 11/0 color C, two 3mm bicones color C, one 4mm bicone color B, one silver 11/0, one 4mm bicone color B, one silver 11/0, one 4mm bicone color A, one silver 11/0, and the pendant. Pick up the beads for the other side of the pendant in reverse order as previously stated. On the other end of the beadwork, stitch down through the bottom bead of the 5th column and up through the 4th column.

6. Stitch down through the top bead of the fifth column and through the added strand to the other side. Stitch up though the top bead of the fifth column. If desired, repeat the thread path to reinforce.

7. The thread ends are now next to each other. Tie a square knot, weave in and cut.

figure 1

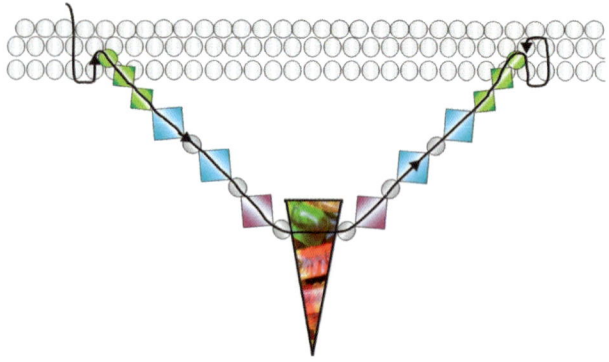

figure 2

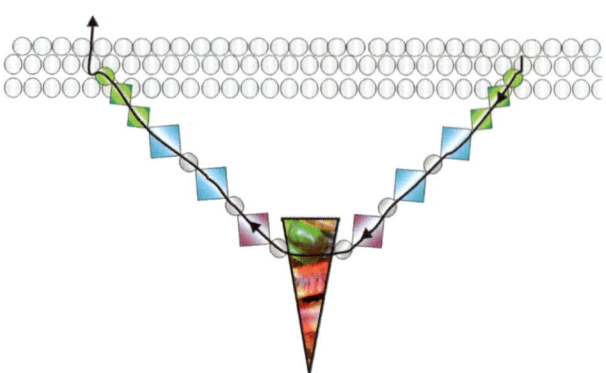

figure 3

Project 6 – Standard Fringe

When fringe is constructed from a straight edge, its intrinsic design is a grid. This allows you to use graph paper for loom or square stitch to create a design within your fringe. The end sequences in the project are managed so that each fringe has the room to hang straight down, not moved or pushed by another strands end bead.

Supplies:

9 grams seed beads 11/0 white opaque
2 grams seed beads 11/0 pastel pink ceylon
2 grams seed beads 11/0 color lined green
2 grams seed beads 11/0 blue opaque matte
2 grams seed beads 11/0 red opaque
1 gram seed beads 6/0 white opaque
25 each beads round 4mm red opaque
13 each beads round 6mm red opaque
30 each beads round 8m red opaque
9 each beads puffed heart 10mm red opaque
1 each bead tube 5x80mm pink transparent
Standard beading kit (page 92) plus a 4inch needle
Standard necklace kit (page 92) silver

Steps:

1. Create a ladder with 31 columns using the instructions for Basic 2-bead Ladder Stitch on page 88 with the white 11/0 seed beads.

2. Cut 6 yards of thread and put on a stop bead with a 3 yard tail to use the Half-thread Method (page 87). Start in the center, stitching down into the 16th column (center). Create that fringe and fringes to the right. Use the tail thread for the left fringes. See the chart below for the count and bead colors to use. (The top strip is shown above the fringe beads). Do not end the threads.

3. Use the current thread on the right. Stitch down through the previous column and up through the current column to lock the thread. Pick up one 4mm round and thirteen white 11/0 beads using the stitch path below to create a top loop. Repeat the thread path two more times to reinforce.

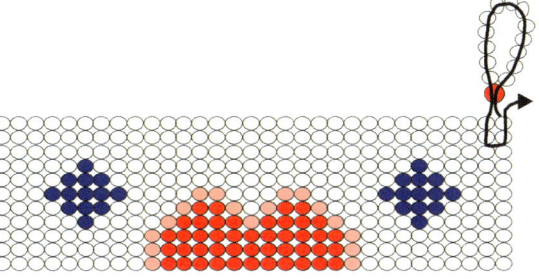

4. Stitch over to the next columns and create another loop using the instructions in the previous step and the thread path below. Continue adding loops until there are four loops on the right. Tie a knot in the thread, weave in and cut.

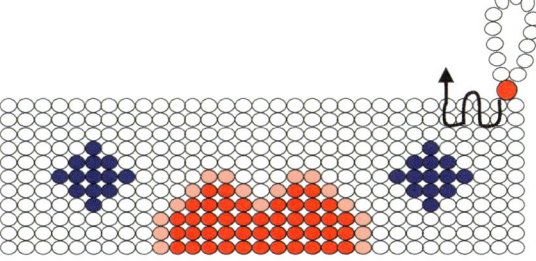

5. Use the current thread on the left and repeat steps 3 and 4 to create 4 more loops on the left.

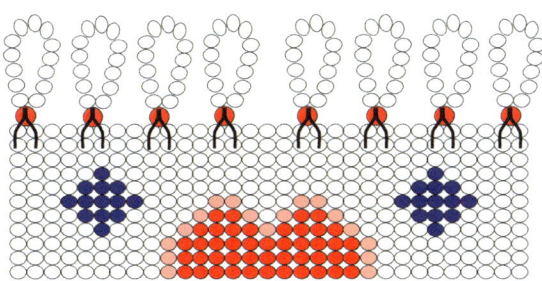

6. Cut 3 yards of thread and put on the 4 inch needle. Move the needle to the center to work doubled thread. Add a stop bead with a 6 inch tail. Pick up one 6/0 bead. Pick up one 11/0 pink and one 8mm round and repeat until there are fourteen 8mm beads in the strand. Pick up one 11/0 pink, one 6mm round, one 11/0 pink, one heart, one 11/0 pink, one 6mm round, one 11/0 pink, one 8mm round and one 11/0 pink.

7. Stitch through the tube bead. String the top loops of the fringe beadwork onto the tube bead. Pick up beads for the other side of the strand as in step 6 in mirror image ending with a 6/0 bead. Pick up nine 11/0 white beads and stitch through them again to create a loop. Stitch back through the entire strand to return to the starting point. Remove the stop bead and pick up nine 11/0 white beads. Stitch through those beads again to create a loop and adjust the tension in the strand. Tie a square knot with the tail threads and needle threads. Put a needle on each of the tail threads and stitch down 2 inches into the neck strand. Pull them to pull the knot into the 6/0 bead. Cut the ends. Use the needle thread to stitch around the loop one more time and stitch down the strand though the tube bead.

8. Pick up eight 11/0 white beads and stitch down into the last column. Pick up three 11/0 white beads and stitch through the previously added bead skipping the nearest two. Stitch back through the tube. Repeat on the other side and continue through the tube and through the strand on the other side up to the end loop. Cut the thread near the needle to split into two threads. Stitch around the loop with one of the threads. Tie a square knot with the ends. Stitch one end two inches down into the strand. Stitch around the loop one more time with the other thread then 2 inches down the strand. Cut the ends.

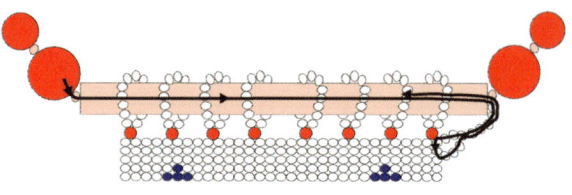

9. Use pliers and jump rings to attach the clasp.

Project 7 – Standard Fringe

Fringe is perfect for creating stunning earrings. You can create these earrings as photographed or you can create the base and earring top as detailed below and substitute the beads, colors and fringe designs from other projects.

Supplies:
3 grams seed beads 11/0 silver luster
1 gram bugle beads twisted 6mm silver metallic
10 each crystal bead bicone 3mm light rose
2 each crystal bead bicone 4mm light rose
10 each round bead crackle glass 4mm pink
10 each round glass beads 4mm silver
10 each round glass beads 6mm pink speckle
2 each ear wires fish hook type silver
Standard beading kit (page 92)

Steps:
1. Use 1 1/2 yards of thread and create a ladder with five columns of two silver 11/0 seed beads using the instructions for Basic 2-bead Ladder Stitch on page 88 except do not weave in the needle or tail thread.
2. Stitch up the first column (knot is on the bottom of the strip) and pick up twelve seed beads and stitch over to the other side. Add the fringe according to the fringe chart (column 5). (figure 1) Stitch through the top loop to the other side and down the first column and add the fringe.

(figure 2.) Stitch down the next column and add the fringe for column 2. (figure 3)

3. Pick up two seed beads and stitch through the top loop beads skipping the first and last two beads in the loop. (figure 4) Pick up two seed beads and stitch down the fourth column. Add the fringe for the fourth column and stitch down the center (third) column. (figure 5) Add the center column fringe and stitch down the next column. The needle and tail threads are now next to each other. Use them to tie a square knot. Weave in the ends and cut.

4. Repeat all steps for the second earring. For each earring, use the pliers to twist open the loop on the ear wires, insert the beaded loop, then close.

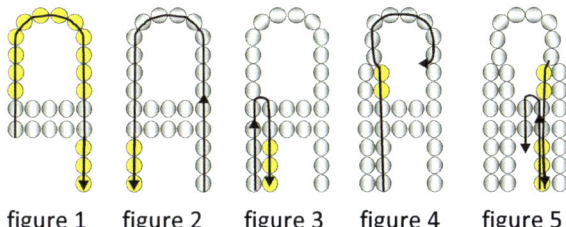

figure 1   figure 2   figure 3   figure 4   figure 5

figure 6

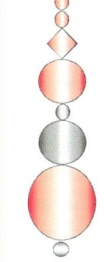

Three pink 11/0 beads
3mm bicone
4mm round pink
Silver 11/0
4mm silver
6mm round
Silver 11/0 (turn bead)

Fringe Chart:
Column	count
center	one silver 11/0, one bugle, one silver 11/0, one 4mm bicone, one silver 11/0, one bugle, three silver 11/0, plus end sequence
2,4	15 silver 11/0 plus end sequence
1,5	12 silver 11/0 plus end sequence

Project 8 – Standard Fringe

The process and technique are basically the same as the previous project, but the use of different colors and profile for the fringe design creates a dramatically different look.

Supplies:

1 gram seed beads 11/0 white opaque
1 gram seed beads 11/0 black opaque
1 gram bugle beads 6mm white opaque
1 gram bulge beads 6mm black opaque
6 each round glass bead 6mm white opaque
6 each round glass beads 4mm white opaque
6 each acrylic dice bead 7mm corner cut white with black dots
4 each round glass bead 6mm black opaque
4 each round glass beads 4mm black opaque
4 each acrylic dice bead 7mm corner cut black with white dots
2 each ear wires fish hook type silver
Standard beading kit (page 92)

Steps

1. Use the 11/0, and bugle beads with the instructions for the 3-bead ladder stitch page 88 and create a five column strip except do not weave in the thread ends. Start with three columns of white and then 2 columns of black.

2. Do steps 2 through 4 for Project 7 to create the earrings. On the top loop of twelve, use six white beads and six black beads. Use the fringe chart that follows.

End Sequence

- 4mm round
- Dice bead
- 6mm round
- 11/0 seed bead (turn bead)

Fringe chart:

Column	color	count plus end sequence
1	white	3
2	white	7
3	white	11
4	black	15
5	black	19

Supplies:

5 grams seed beads 11/0 crystal color lined aqua
15 grams seed bead triangles 8/0 crystal AB
20 grams seed bead triangles 5/0 crystal color lined purple (color A)
20 grams seed bead triangles 5/0 crystal color lined fuchsia (color B)
20 grams seed bead triangles 5/0 crystal color lined teal (color C)
1 each toggle clasp silver
4 each jump rings 5mm silver
Standard beading kit (page 92)

Project 9 - Standard Fringe

The previous projects put the lush nature of standard fringe on display. This project brings home the point that fringe can be short and it is still wonderful. Fringe can be constructed off of an edge but also on the surface of beadwork like in this project

Steps:

Make the base:

1. Cut 2 ½ yards of thread. Put on a needle and move the thread to the middle to work with doubled thread.

2. Pick up ten 11/0 and two 8/0 seed beads. Move down the thread leaving a six inch tail. Stitch through the beads again and pull to create a circle. Tie a square knot with the tail threads and needle thread.

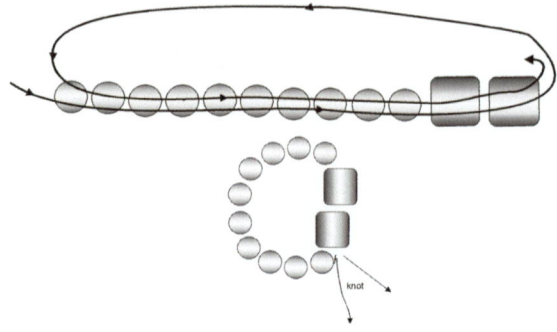

3. Pick up one 8/0 seed bead and stitch through the 8/0 bead on the circle. Pick up one 8/0 seed bead and stitch through the bead previously added. Repeat until you have the length you want remembering to account for the end loops and the jump rings and clasp that will be added later.

4. Pick up ten 11/0 beads. Stitch through the two 8/0 seed beads on the end to create a circle. Go through the loop again to strengthen ending in the middle of the two 8/0 seed beads. Leave the thread end to be used later.

Embellish with Standard Fringe:

5. Cut 2 yards of thread and put a needle on to work single thread. Go to the end of the bracelet with the needle thread. Stitch through one 8/0 seed bead, starting in the middle and stitch out to the edge, leaving a tail of six inches. Use this tail and the previous needle thread and tie a square knot. Weave in the thread ends and cut.

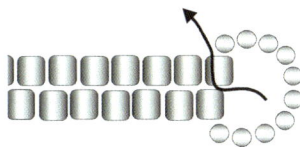

6. Each fringe consists of two 11/0, one 5/0 and one 11/0 as the turn bead. Each row has three fringes on it: One on the top (figure 1). One in the center (figure 2) and then one on the bottom (figure 3) stitching up to set up for the next row. For the first row, use color A, then color B, and end with color C. On the next row, start with color B, then C and end with color A. For the next row, start with color C, then A, end with color B. Repeat that pattern across the bracelet base. See "Adding new Thread" when the current thread has approximately 6 to 9 inches left.

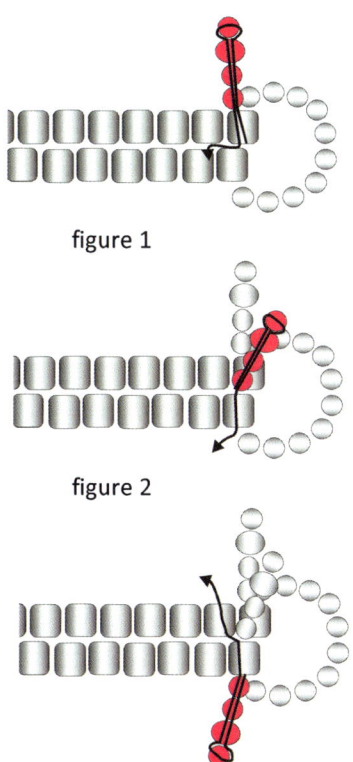

figure 1

figure 2

figure 3

7. When you reach the end of the bracelet, tie knots in the thread, weave in and cut. See Finish with Findings on page 90 and attach the clasp.

Adding a new thread:

Add new thread when there is 6 to 9 inches left on the old thread. Start after a side fringe and stitch to the middle of the base (see red dot). Cut 2 yards thread and put on a needle to work single thread. Stitch from the center of the next set out to the edge and through the previous row out to the edge. This is the new thread ready to continue. Pull the new thread until there is a nine inch tail. Take the old needle and new tail threads and tie a square knot. Weave the ends in and cut. Continue adding fringe.

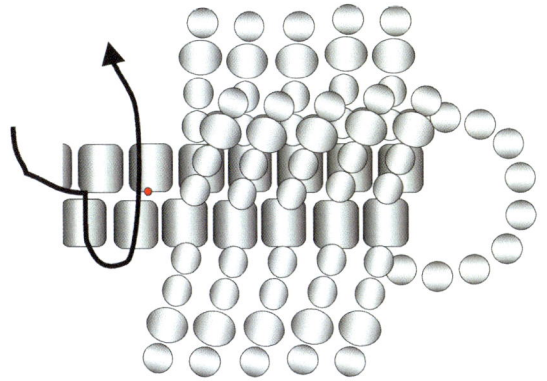

Backside view

Chapter 4: Loop Fringe

Loop fringe is the easiest and fastest fringe to create. This fringe has a loop on the bottom so it doesn't hang straight down and has an organic, free-flowing appearance. It is especially useful when you want to create a chunky looking fringe.

Loop fringe is created with doubled thread. There are two alternatives when attaching loop fringe into beadwork. One is to attach the sides of the loop into sequential beads (below left) and the other is to attach both sides into one bead (below right). It is easier to achieve proper tension with the first method and the fringe will lay flatter.

1. Exit the beadwork where you want to attach the fringe strand.

2. Pick up beads for one side of the loop, the bottom, and then the other side of the loop. Move the beads up the thread until they are next to the beadwork.

3. Stitch up into the beadwork and pull on the thread to adjust the tension. Getting the proper tension in loop fringe is slightly different from standard fringe. If the fringe is heavy, chunky or has lots of other beads besides seed beads, then the technique for tension is the same as standard fringe. First, pull to achieve the perfect tension. Then pull just a little tighter. The more seed beads in the strand, the more tension to add beyond the perfect tension. However, when the loop is short and/or consists solely of seed beads, too much tension will make the fringe stick out and not hang properly. Accordingly, it is better to just pull to the proper tension and not any tighter.

Tip: Doubled thread is easier to manage when you regularly adjust your thread. Run your fingers down the thread moving toward the needle to remove twists and reposition the needle to the center.

How to design loop fringe:

- Select beads, both seeds and others you may want to use in the fringe. Thread a needle with a 1/2 yard of thread and put on a stop bead. Use this to design your fringe.

- The loop at the bottom will form a "U" shape so the final length as the fringe as it hangs will be shorter than one half of the total length.

- The fringe will hang straighter when there are heavy beads at the bottom, otherwise the loop will be wider, more open.

- The loop will be more open at the bottom if the bottom bead is wide.

- You can design the fringe using the same concepts as described for standard fringe using a count of seed beads and an end sequence as discussed on page 16 including the decrease considerations and testing.

In the photos above, one side of the loop is different from the other side, but each loop is like the other loops. Notice also the use of large (6mm plus) beads throughout the fringe strand creating a chunky appearance.

In the photos above, not only is one side of the loop different from the other side, but each loop is different from the other loops.

- While the sides of loop fringe are equal length, they do not need to be the same bead sequence. The right side can have one design while the left is another. Pick up beads for one side then use a ruler to measure it. Add the bottom sequence and pick up beads for the other side using a ruler to measure. Add or remove beads until it is the same length as the previous side. See also the Variation on page 38 for alternating the spacing.

- Loop fringe on beadwork that is curved requires an adjustment to the length of the side of the loop that is farthest from center. This adjustment is typically one to two seed beads and allows the loop bottom to hang properly. At some point the curve of the edge designated in red in the figure right lifts one side of the loop. The bottom center of the loop will not hang properly unless you add one or two beads on the upper side of the loop as in the figure. When you bead along a curved area, change the count of the beads on that side of the loop.

37

- Bottom beads that are flat with a side drill will lay better at the bottom of the loop. Top drilled beads that are not side drilled will hang sideways or will twist the loop such that one side will be in front of the other side.

- Loop fringe strands hang more neatly when each side is stitched into sequential beads in the beadwork. This requires two entry/exit points on the beadwork, an even number of beads. If, however you need to cover an odd number, then there is one bead in the center. Here are three options for this situation.

Option 1: Create a loop into one bead

Option 2: Create a standard fringe strand in the center bead surrounded by loops

Option 3: Create a standard fringe inside a loop created around the center

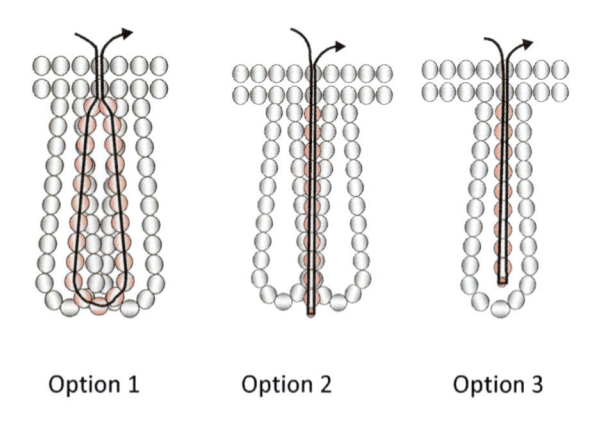

Option 1   Option 2   Option 3

- Many of the design considerations used in Standard Fringe also apply to Loop Fringe. Colors can be shaded down the fringe or across fringe strands (as in the photos below). You can alternate the use of large end beads (on one strand, then skip on the next one or more strands), and use different beads in the strands or alternate to create a pattern.

- You can use the same beads but vary the spacing within the loop. Instructions for the "Loop Fringe variation – Alternating spacing on the sides" follow:

a. Use doubled thread and start in the center.

b. Pick up five seed beads and one other bead. Repeat until you have the length you desire. Then pick up the bottom bead(s).

c. For the other side of the loop, start with eight seed beads, then one other bead. This will position the other beads on this side of the strand in between the other beads on the first side. Pick up five seed beads and one other bead until you have one less other bead than on the first side. Fill to the top so that the center bottom bead is at the center, generally seven to nine beads. The illustration on the left is when the center is two edge beads, while the example on the right is when the edge center is through one bead.

d. Repeat b and c for subsequent fringes. After the center fringe is done, be sure to stitch the subsequent side loops in mirror image as illustrated. The center is the yellow. Notice how the side loops (orange and blue) are mirror images of each other.

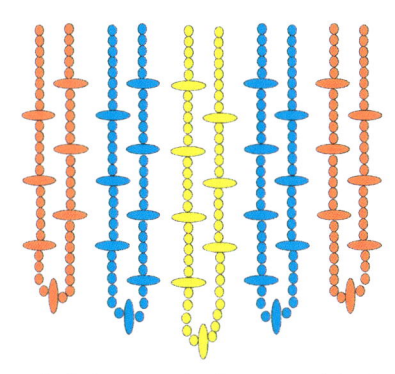

e. For a "U" shape at the bottom of the fringe, do the center loop plus one or two loops on each side the same length. Reduce the bead count on subsequent loops.

f. For a "V" shape at the bottom of the fringe, do the center loop start and then reduce the bead count on each subsequent loop.

g. To shorten the fringes reduce the bead count from the bottom, not the top as with typical fringe techniques. This is because you need at least 5 seed beads between the edge and the other bead or the fringe will be too crowded near the edge and won't lay right. So, eliminate the seed beads at the bottom, usually one or two beads. When the elimination gets to the other bead, estimate the seed bead equivalent of the space used by the other bead, usually two or more and adjust as needed. See illustration for example.

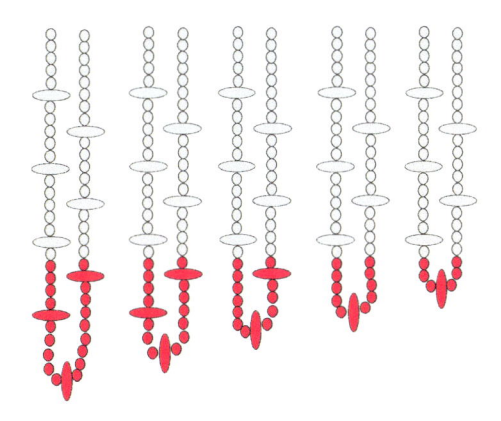

Project 1 - Loop Fringe:

This project emphasizes that loop fringe can be dramatic even with short loops. Some of the loops are created entirely of seeds beads while others have different beads on the bottom of the loop.

Supplies:

1 gram seed beads 15/0 medium cream luster
18 grams seed beads 11/0 medium cream luster
4 grams twin 2-hole seed beads light peach pearl
28 to 33 each round pearls 6mm cream
59 to 63 each round pearls 4mm cream
30 each round pearls 3mm cream
2 each safety pins
Standard beading kit (page 92)
Standard necklace kit (page 92) gold

Steps:

Create the base:-

1. Cut 3 yards of thread and put a needle on to work single thread. Add a stop bead with a nine inch tail.

2. Pick up nine 11/0 beads and move to the stop bead. Stitch through the beads again and pull to create a circle. Stitch through the beads one more time to reinforce. Remove the stop bead and use the needle and tail thread to tie a square knot. Leave the tail thread for use later and with the needle thread, stitch through two more beads away from the knot.

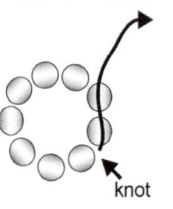

3. Pick up two seed beads and stitch through the previous column. Pull and stitch through the new column again.

4. Pick up two 11/0, one 6mm, four 11/0, one 4mm, four 11/0, and one 4mm. Stitch up through two beads in the previous section. Pull and stitch through the added beads to the first 4mm bead.

5. Pick up three 11/0, five twins, seven 11/0, one 6mm and two 11/0 beads. Stitch down through the two beads above the 4mm bead on the previous section. Stitch through all the added beads again, then stitch through the bottom section again stopping two beads before the 6mm bead.

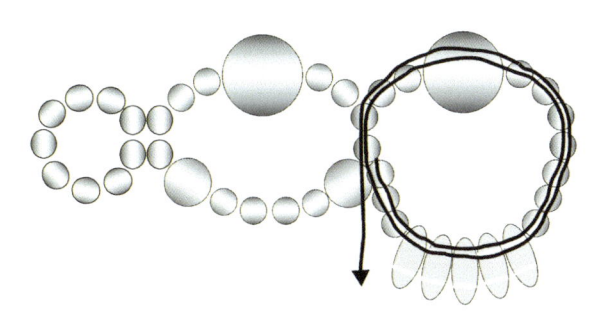

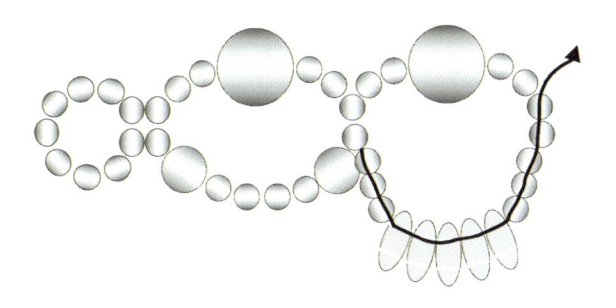

6. Repeat steps 4 and 5 until you have the desired length (twelve or more times) ending with step 4. Pick up two 11/0 beads and stitch down through two beads of the previous section. Stitch up through the added beads. Pick up seven 11/0 beads and stitch up through two beads of the previous section. Pull to create a circle. Stitch around the circle two more times to reinforce. Leave the thread end for use later.

Add the fringe;-

7. Cut 4 yards of thread and thread a needle on. Move the needle to the center to work doubled thread. Identify the center five sections with the twin beads on the bottom. Put a safety pin in the loop of the first and the loop of the fifth of the center five.

8. At one end, stitch through the 4mm bead and the next four 11/0 beads. Pull until there is a six inch tail. Use the thread end left over from the steps to create the base and the tail of the new thread to tie a square knot. Weave in the ends and cut. Pick up four 11/0 beads and stitch through the bottom hole of the nearest twin.

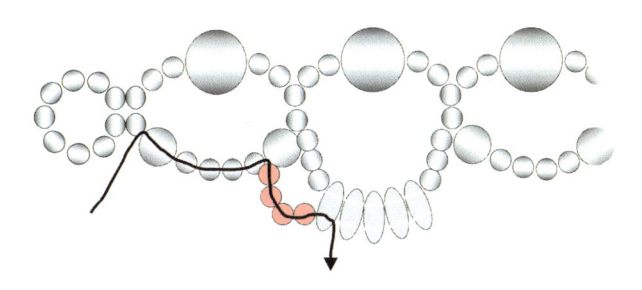

9. Pick up fifteen 11/0 beads and stitch through the twin, entering on the other side. Pick up one 15/0 bead and stitch through the next twin. Repeat across the strip of twin beads using the bead counts as illustrated. Pick up four 11/0 seed beads and stitch through the four seed beads between the 4mm beads in the next section. Pick up four 11/0 beads and stitch through the nearest twin in the next section. Repeat this step until you reach the center five sections.

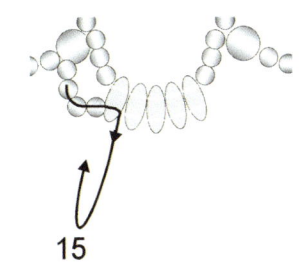

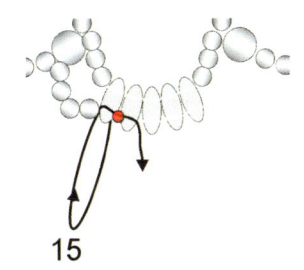

15   15

41

15　　15
19　19
　23

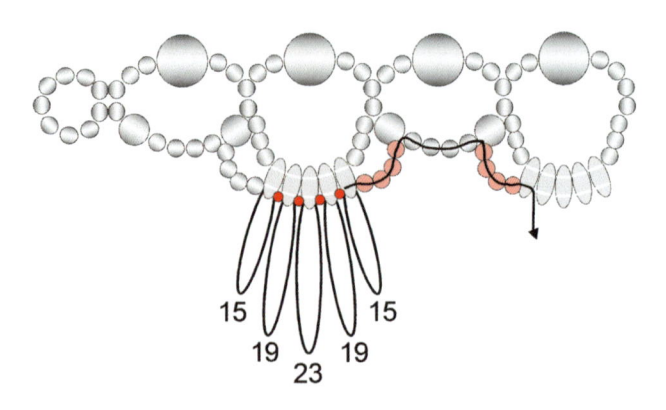

Tip: Loop fringe made entirely of seed beads can easily become too stiff when there is too much tension in the thread. Be careful that you do not pull too tightly. As you finish a loop, review the previous loop to ensure you did not inadvertently change the tension in that loop as you constructed the current loop.

10. Use the procedures in the previous step with the charts below to construct the fringe on the center five sections. These loops use 11/0 seed beads on the side and other size beads on the bottom. Use the chart below for the count of beads on the sides of loop.

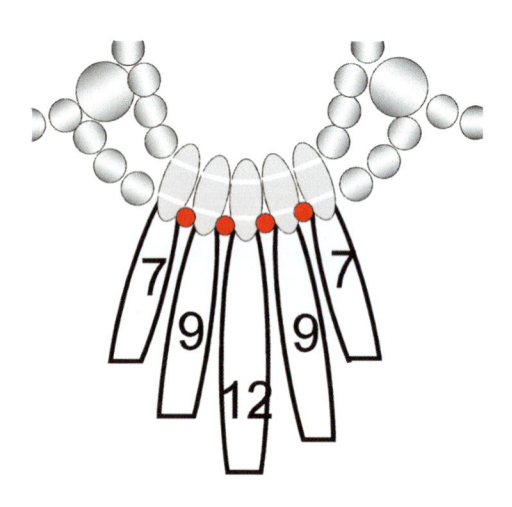

7　　　7
9　9
　12

Use this chart for the bottom of the loop:
1st and 5th section　　One 4mm
2nd and 4th sections　One 3mm, one 4mm and one 3mm
Center (3rd section)　One 3mm, one 4mm, one 6mm, one 4mm and one 3mm

11. Repeat step 9 to the end of the necklace.

12. Use the needle thread and thread end from the steps to create the base to tie a square knot. Weave the ends in and cut.

13. Use pliers with the jump rings to attach the hook to one side and the chain to the other side. Add beads on the head pin, trim and attach to the end of the chain.

Adding new thread:
1. End the old thread after a section is finished, pick up four beads and stitch around the next section as illustrated in blue.

2. Cut 4 yards of thread and put a needle on. Move the needle to the center to work with doubled thread. Stitch down through the two seed beads next to the old thread plus the 4mm and four 11/0 beads as illustrated in red.

3. Use the old needle thread and new tail to tie a square knot. Weave in the ends pulling the knot into the bead holes and cut the ends. Resume according to the instructions with the new thread.

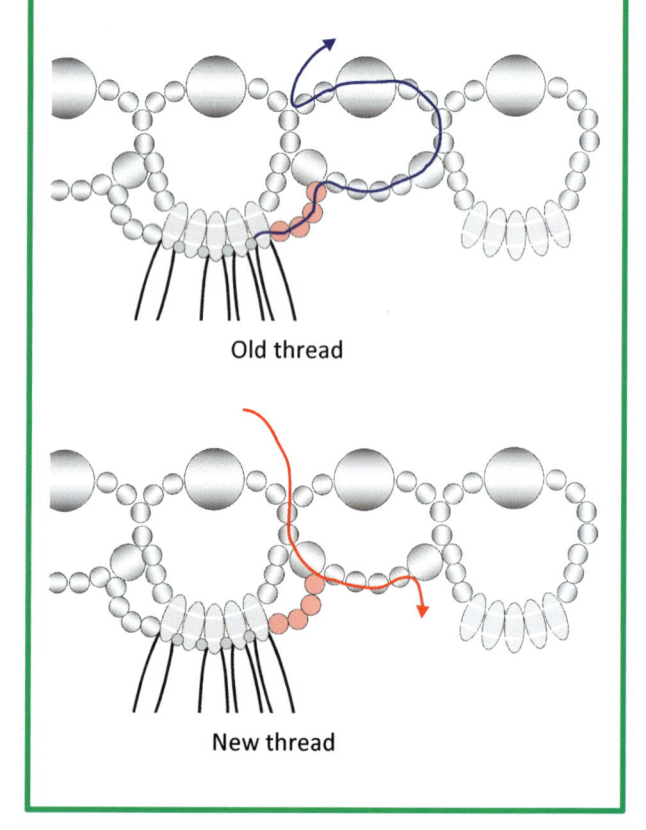

Old thread

New thread

Project 2 – Loop Fringe:

This project showcases loops that include other beads in the sides of the loops and both sides are the same. This project uses the same base as the previous project and shows how to adapt that project into a bib style.

Supplies:

1 gram seed beads 15/0 metallic bright gold
7 grams seed beads 11/0 blue color lined purple
1 gram seed beads 11/0 metallic bright gold
1 gram seed beads 11/0 dark aqua transparent
1 gram seed beads 6/0 dark aqua transparent
2 grams twin 2-hole seed beads lilac transparent pearl
50 each fire polish beads 3mm light cobalt
50 each fire polish beads 4mm green
62 each fire polish beads 4mm dark aqua
12 each round beads 6mm dark aqua
22 to 26 each round beads 8mm dark aqua
50 each dagger beads 3x11 mm blue zircon
25 each dagger beads 4x15mm cobalt
Standard beading kit (page 92)
Standard necklace kit (page 92) gold

Steps:

1. Cut 2 yards of thread and put a needle on to work single thread. Add a stop bead with a nine inch tail.

2. Pick up four purple 11/0 beads and move down to stop bead. Stitch through the first two again and pull to create two columns. Stitch through the next column.

3. Do Steps 4 and 5 on page 41 until you have five sections with the twin bead loops and end with step 4. Use the purple and gold 11/0 beads and the 4mm dark aqua fire polish beads as illustrated below. Leave the thread ends for use later.

4. Cut 5 yards of thread and put a needle on it. Move the needle to the middle to work with doubled thread. Use the thread path and processes in Steps 8 and 9 on page 41 to create the fringes. The loops include the purple 11/0 beads on each side of the loop using the counts indicated below. The loops use the same count within the section and all sections use the same bottom loop sequence as illustrated below. Use the old and new thread ends on each side to tie square knots. Weave in the ends and cut.

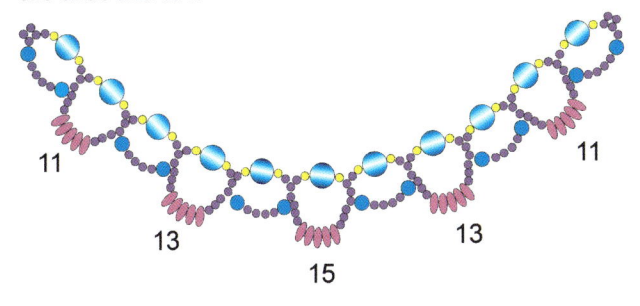

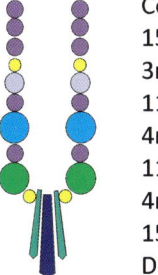

Count
15/0 gold
3mm
11/0 purple
4mm dark aqua
11/0 purple
4mm green
15/0 gold
Daggers (zircon, cobalt, zircon)

5. Use the 8mm and gold 11/0 beads with the instructions for the Necklace Strand with Side Attachment on page 89 and create the necklace strands. Use the dark aqua 6/0 and 11/0 seed beads for the end loops.

Project 3 – Loop Fringe:

In the previous projects, Loop Fringe was used to hang down from the bottom of beadwork. In this project, the fringe is done on the sides and also embellishes the surface of beadwork. This bracelet uses short loop fringe in a rainbow of colors with seed beads only to create the loops

Supplies:
5 grams seed beads 11/0 matte fuchsia
5 grams seed beads 11/0 matte orange
5 grams seed beads 11/0 matte yellow
5 grams seed beads 11/0 matte lime
5 grams seed beads 11/0 matte turquoise
5 grams seed beads 11/0 matte lavender
10 grams seed beads 6/0 rocaille or triangle, clear AB
1 each toggle clasp
4 jump rings
Standard beading kit (page 92)

Steps:
Make the base:
1. Do Steps 1 through 4 on page 34 except use the 6/0 beads where the steps call for an 8/0 bead and use the fuchsia beads for the 11/0 beads.

Embellish with Loop Fringe:
2. Cut 3 yards of thread and put a needle on. Move the needle to the middle to work with doubled thread. Go to the end of the bracelet with the needle thread. Stitch through one 6/0 seed bead, starting in the middle and stitch out to the edge, leaving a tail of six inches. Use this tail and the previous needle thread and tie a square knot. Weave in all of the thread ends and cut.

figure 1

For the next steps, start with the first color listed (fuchsia) and continue with that color through step 6. Each time you repeat this series of steps, go to the next color on the list for that set. At the end of the list, restart with the first color (fuchsia). See "Adding new Thread" page 45 when the current thread has approximately six inches left.

3. Pick up ten 11/0 seed beads and move the beads all the way toward the bracelet base. Stitch back into the same base bead to create the side loop fringe. (figure 2)

4. Pick up ten 11/0 seed beads and move the beads all the way toward the bracelet base. Stitch through the same base bead again entering on the other side of the bead. Stitch through that bead and the next base bead in the row. Pull to create a top loop fringe. (figure 3)

44

5. Pick up ten 11/0 seed beads and move the beads all the way toward the bracelet base. Stitch through the same base bead again, entering on the other side of the bead and out to the edge. Pull to create a top loop fringe. (figure 4)

6. Pick up ten 11/0 seed beads and move the beads all the way toward the bracelet base. Stitch back into the same base bead and through the base bead in the next row to the other side. Pull to create a side loop fringe. (figure 5)

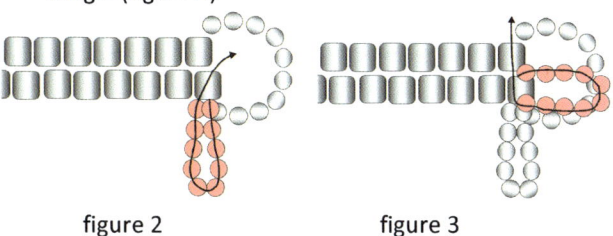

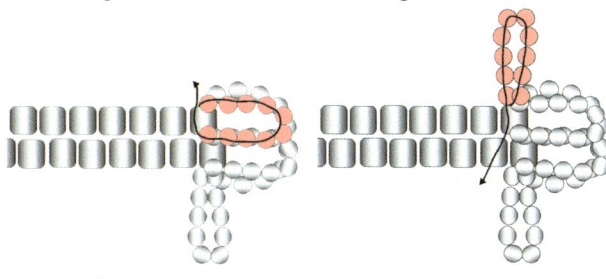

figure 2   figure 3

figure 4   figure 5

7. Repeat steps 3 to 6 across the bracelet base. When done, tie a knot, weave the ends in and cut. Use jump rings to attach the clasp on each end.

Adding new thread: Add new thread when you have approximately six inches left. Start after a side fringe (ends in the middle of the base, see red dot). Cut 2 to 3 yards thread and put on a needle to work single thread. Stitch from the center of the next row out to the edge, and back to the center where the tail thread is (red dot). This is the new thread ready to continue. Pull new thread till there is a six inch tail. Take the old needle and new tail and tie a square knot. Weave the ends in and cut. Continue adding loop fringe.

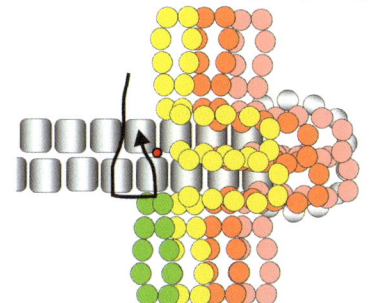

Backside view

45

Project 4 – Loop Fringe:

The loops in this project use one sequence for the beads for one side of the loop and a different sequence for the other side of the loop. This project also uses one of the methods for dealing with an odd count of edge beads when creating loop fringe (see pg. 38 for examples).

Supplies:

2 grams seed beads 11/0 bright gold metallic
8 grams 4mm cube seed beads gold metallic
21 each rondelle bead 6x2.5mm emerald AB
13 each round bead 4mm light amethyst
18 each fire polish 4mm blue/green two tone
6 each diamond bicone 5mm light amethyst
7 each square bead 5x7mm fuchsia/green two tone
34 each faceted harlequin rectangle bead 8x4mm light blue AB
1 each flat uneven round 15mm blue with geometric rainbow coating
Standard beading kit (page 92)
Standard necklace kit (page 92) gold

Steps:

Create the base using Square Stitch

1. Cut 2 yards of thread and put a needle on to work single thread. Add a stop bead with a six inch tail.

2. Pick up two cube beads and move down to the stop bead. Stitch through the first bead again and line the beads up side by side. * Pick up 2 cube beads and stitch down one cube bead into the next column and up into the current column. * Repeat the steps * to * until it is a total of eight beads tall. Pick up two cube beads and stitch down one cube bead into the next column. Stitch up one bead in the current column, then up one bead into the next column.

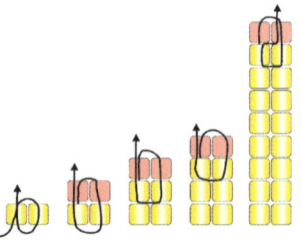

3. Pick up one cube bead and stitch into the previous column and again through the current column. Repeat until there are a total of nine columns. Knot the thread ends, weave in and cut.

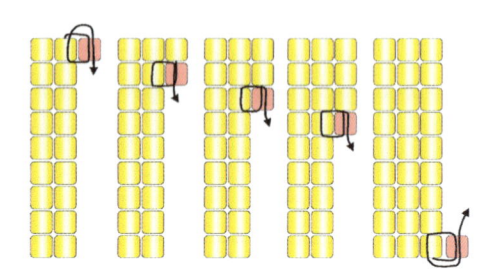

Add the fringe

4. Cut 2 ½ yards of thread and put a needle on. Move the needle to the center to work with doubled thread. Add a stop bead with a six inch tail.

5. On the left side, stitch down three cube beads to the bottom. Create the loop fringes according to the fringe chart below. Review page 12 for stitching the fringe into a square stitch base. When finished with the fringes, remove the stop bead and knot the tail thread ends, weave in and cut. Use the needle thread in the following steps to add the embellishment.

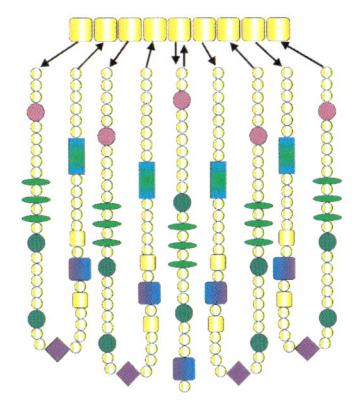

The first loop: three 11/0, one 4mm round , five 11/0, one rondelle, one 11/0 one rondelle, one 11/0 , one rondelle, one 11/0, one 4mm fire polish, five 11/0, one 4mm fire polish, two 11/0, one bicone (bottom center), four 11/0, one cube, one 11/0, one square, one 11/0, one cube, five 11/0, one rectangle, six 11/0.

Second loop: same as first loop except add two 11/0 at the beginning and end.

Center fringe (standard fringe): two 11/0, one 4mm round, seven 11/0, one 4mm fire polish, one 11/0, one rondelle, one 11/0, one rondelle, one 11/0, one rondelle, three 11/0, one 4mm fire polish, three 11/0 one square, one 11/0 (turn bead).

Third loop: Same as second loop in mirror image.

Last Loop: Same as first loop in mirror image.

> **Tip:** When creating an original design using a standard fringe in the center, stitch all of the loop fringes first and the center fringe last. This will help you judge the length to use for the center fringe.

Add the necklace and embellishment

6. Continue using the thread from adding the fringe and stitch through the cubes beads in a circle as illustrated. This will help hold the tension in the final loop fringe. Then stitch up and out the top row, in the third column.

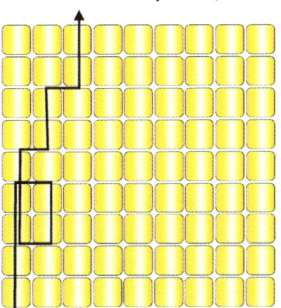

7. Pick up twelve 11/0, one 4mm fire polish, two 11/0, one 15mm flat round, and three 11/0 beads. Stitch back up through the 15mm bead to create a Picot end (page 10) and pull to adjust the tension. Pick up two 11/0, one 4mm fire polish, and twelve 11/0 beads. Stitch down through the cube bead three columns in from the other side. Stitch through the cube beads like in the previous step to lock the tension. Knot the thread, weave in and cut.

8. Use the chart on the left with the instructions for the Necklace Strand with Side Attachment on page 89 to create the necklace strands.

47

Project 5 - Loop Fringe:

This project uses a top and side drilled bead at the bottom of the loop with different spacing of beads on the sides of the loop.

Supplies:
12 grams seed beads 11/0 silver luster
1 strand 35 inch glass chip beads blue
1 gram seed beads 6/0 grey peal
8 grams 4mm cube seed beads gold metallic
56 each round beads 6mm light blue rainbow
40 each round beads 8mm light blue rainbow
16 each leaf top/side drilled drop beads silver coated clear
1 each flower pendant 35mm antique silver
Standard beading kit (page 92)
Standard necklace kit (page 92) silver
    Plus: 4 each jump rings 5mm silver
2 each two-hole necklace findings silver
19 inches flexible beading wire .019

Steps:
Create the base -
1. Create a ladder with 32 columns of two silver 11/0 seed beads using the instructions for Basic 2-bead Ladder Stitch on page 88.

Create the fringe -
2. Cut 6 yards of thread. Put a needle on each end and move each of them 1 ½ yards (1/4 of the total yardage) from the ends to work with doubled thread using the Half Thread Method (page 87). Stitch down in the seventeenth column from the left and pull until there is 6 inches left on the short end of the thread. Use the other needle and stitch down the 16th column again pulling until there is 6 inches left on the short end of the thread. Reposition the needles as needed. Use the two short ends and tie a square knot. Weave in the thread ends and cut. Wrap the needle thread to the left in a sticky note and set aside to use later.

3. See the instructions on page 39 for the loop fringe variation – alternating spacing on the sides. Use the chips as the "other bead" for alternating with the 11/0 beads and the leaf drop for the bottom. The center two fringes are the same length with a decrease of two on the next fringes (loop 7 and 10) and a decrease of three on the subsequent fringes. Note also the adjustment on the top of the outside edge of the final loop. Create the loops from the center to the right. Knot the thread, weave in and cut. Unwrap the other needle and thread from the sticky note. Turn the beadwork over so you can work adding fringe from left to right and create in mirror image.

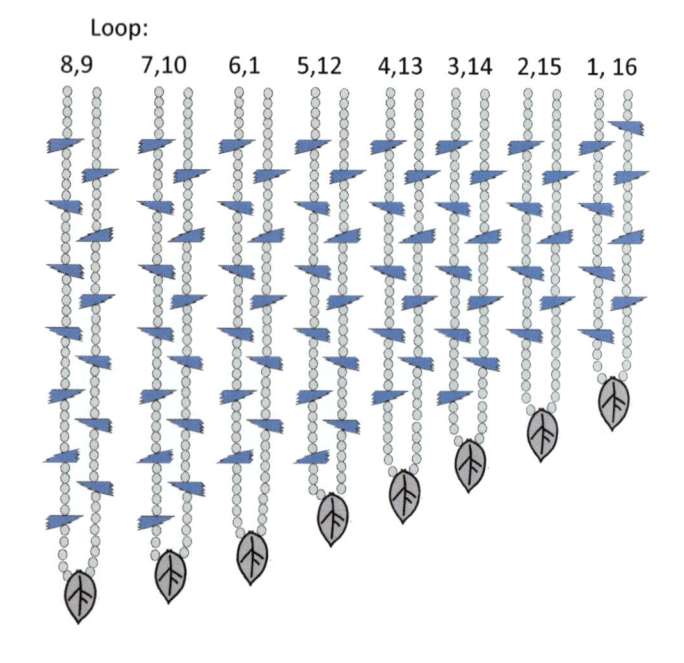

Loop:
8,9   7,10   6,1   5,12   4,13   3,14   2,15   1, 16

figure 1

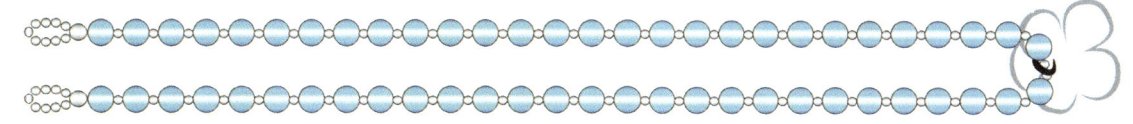

figure 2

Create the necklace strands:

4. Use the 8mm round 11/0 grey beads and instructions for the Necklace Strand with Side Attachment on page 89 and create the necklace strands. (figure 1)

5. Use the flexible beading wire and the 6mm beads, 11/0 grey seed beads and the pendant with the instructions for Stringing with Flexible Beading Wire page 89 to create the other necklace strand. (figure 2)

Or use cupolini coral:

Project 6:

Loop fringe attached to the side creates a dynamic look for these beautiful earrings.

Supplies:

8 grams seed beads 11/0 light orange transparent
5 grams seed beads 3.5-3.7 4mm cubes green color lined orange
5 grams fringe drop beads 4x3.4mm lime rainbow
2 each metal drops 8x30mm teardrop side drilled gold plated
2 each ear wires fish hook style gold
Standard beading kit (page 92)

Steps:

Create the base -

1. Cut 3 yards of thread and put a needle on. Move the needle to the middle to work with doubled thread. Create a ladder with 8 columns of one cube bead using the instructions for Basic 1-bead Ladder Stitch on page 88 steps 2 through 4; do not stitch back through the strip and cut the thread ends. Continue to use the needle thread in the remaining steps.

2. Add the bottom drop. Pick up eight 11/0 beads, the drop and eight 11/0 beads and stitch through the bottom column. Repeat the stitch path to strengthen. Stitch around through the previous column and end column and then through the previous column again. The following steps will add the fringe and this stitching around the columns will lock the thread tension in the added drop so the loop fringe and drop will not affect each other.

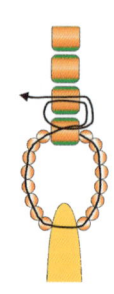

3. Add the fringes. Pick up the number of beads in the fringe chart, the center sequence and the number of beads in the fringe chart. Stitch through the column to the other side and repeat adding the fringe on the other side then stitch through the column and up to the next column. Repeat for all columns.

Fringe Chart:

Column	Count
8 (bottom)	for drop
7	13
6	13
5	13
4	13
3	12
2	11
1 (top)	10

Center sequence: one fringe, one 11/0, one fringe, one 11/0, one fringe

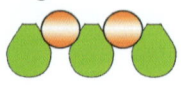

4. Add the top loop. Pick up eight 11/0 beads and stitch through the top column entering the other side. Repeat the thread path two more times to strengthen. Use the needle and tail threads to tie a square knot. Weave in the ends and cut.

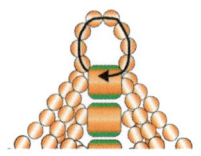

5. Repeat all steps for the second earring. For each earring, use the pliers to twist open the loop on the ear wires, insert the beaded loop, then close.

Designer note: Change colors, bottom drops and the center sequence on the loop fringe for a variety of wonderful earring designs.

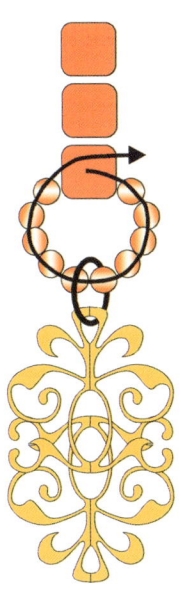

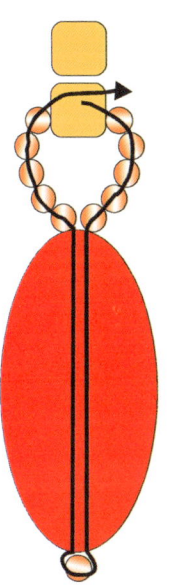

Use charms and stampings attached with a jump ring to a beaded loop. The above earrings include one 4mm crystal bicone as the center sequence.

The above earrings use a 13x10mm oval cloisonné bead as the drop. The center sequence is one fringe drop bead, one 11/0, one 7x3mm dagger, one 11/0, one fringe drop bead.

Chapter 5: Kinky Fringe

Kinky fringe is a variation of standard fringe and has a textured, wild and fun appearance. Use it to add dimension and unpredictability to your beadwork.

Kinky fringe is typically created with single thread. The kinks are created by skipping beads while traveling up the strand and need to be worked with a tight tension.

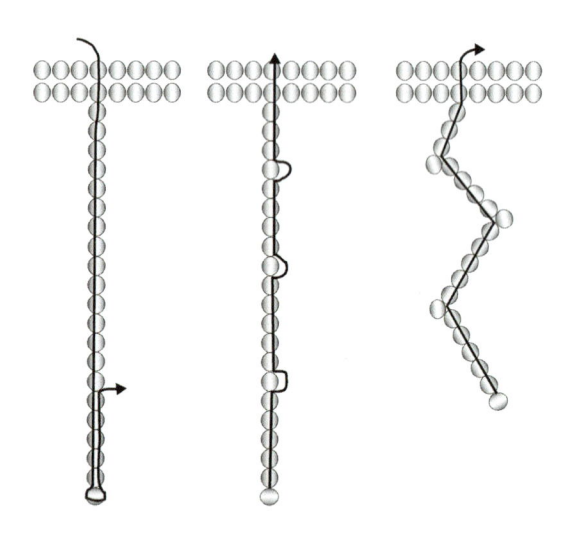

1. Exit the beadwork where you want to attach the fringe strand and pick up beads for fringe plus a turn bead.

2. Skip the bottom turn bead and stitch up the strand to the bead below the first planned kink. Hold the turn bead with one hand and pull on the thread with the other hand to adjust the tension. Use a tight tension.

3. Skip one bead in the strand and stitch up into the strand to the next planned kink. Pull the thread to a tight tension. Repeat all the way up the strand. Pull the tension tight.

Tip: One way to do this fringe is to stitch all the way up to the beadwork, skipping one bead at each kink area and then pull to tighten and create all of the kinks. However, if the strand is long that process doesn't work very well because the thread will become pinched at one kink area and you won't be able to get the proper tension below the pinch. So, when the strand is long and you stitch all the way up do not pull on the needle thread. Instead, start at the bottom and pull the exposed thread at each kink point, working one by one up the strand.

How to design Kinky Fringe:

Select the beads you want to use in the fringe. Typically, this fringe has only seed beads or other small beads (4mm and smaller) without larger beads in an end sequence. You can use large beads in an end sequence but the weight will pull the fringe and reduce the kinky nature of the fringe. Thread a needle with a 1/2 yard of thread and put on a stop bead. Use this to design your fringe.

Key points to consider are:
* Longer fringe is heavier so gravity will have a bigger effect and reduce the kinky appearance.

* Judging the final length can be difficult, there is no formula. The length depends on how many kinks and the length of the intervals between kinks. So, it is important to create a test strand.

* The intervals between the kinks do not have to be uniform. You can experiment with a longer interval at the bottom, reducing as you near the top or vice versa. This will produce a differing blend of kinks.

* Each bead can be the same color (see Project 1). Another alternative is to use a different color seed bead at each kink spot (Project 2 page 56) which emphasizes the kinky appearance. Or vary colors as desired.

* Use different size seed beads in the strand including 15, 11, 8, and 6. Or, include some 2mm or 3mm beads for a chunky, wild appearance. Different sizes can be used inside an interval between kinks or at the kink point.

Kinky Fringe Shorthand:
When you are designing and stitching fringe, it is helpful to take notes so that you can repeat the design again either on another piece or the other side of symmetrical fringe. Here is an easy to read and useful method to take notes for kinky fringe.

15t -4, -3, -2

The first number is how many beads to pick up for the full strand and ends with a turn bead. If there was an end sequence, you can note as "et" for those strands that have an end sequence. If you have more than one end sequence, designate each with a letter and use the appropriate letter in your notes. The subsequent numbers are the count of beads to stitch up the strand to reach the skip bead where the kink will be. After the last number, simply travel the remaining beads in the strand. So, this notation means pick up 15 beads and a turn bead. Skip the turn bead and stitch up four beads into the strand. Skip a bead and travel up the strand for three beads. Skip a bead and travel up two beads in the strand. Skip a bead and travel up the remainder of the strand.

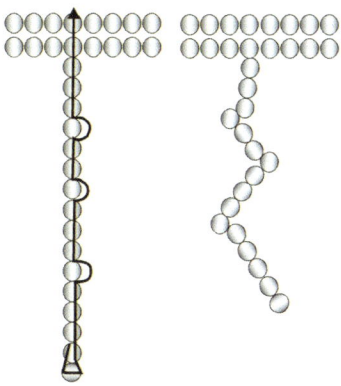

If you are using multiple colors in the strand, designate each color with a letter. For example, red is R, orange is G, yellow is Y. Then " 4R, 4G, 4Y, 4G, 4R, t" means pick up four red, four orange, four yellow, four orange, four red and a turn bead. If the planned kinks are at the color change, then no other notes are needed, just follow the bead colors. If the kinks are different, make notations (for example -6, -7) like the above.

Project 1 – Kinky fringe:
This pin project capitalizes on the random fun appearance of kinky fringe using it as the hair on this stylized doll pin.

Supplies:
2 grams seed beads 11/0 orange color lined
1 each round bead with face 12mm yellow
1 each flat oval bead 15 x 18mm orange foil stripe
2 each fire polish beads 3mm, red transparent
2 each round tube beads 4 x 14mm red transparent
2 each diamond bicone beads 5mm yellow opaque
Standard beading kit (page 92)
1 pin finding, tie tack style with clutch

Steps:

1. Cut 2 yards of thread and put a needle on to work single thread.

2. Stitch into the 12mm round bead leaving a nine inch tail. Stitch through the bead again wrapping the thread around one side of the bead. Repeat. Stitch through the bead again wrapping the thread around the other side of the bead and repeat two more times. Use the needle thread and tail thread and tie a square knot, leaving the tail thread to weave in later.

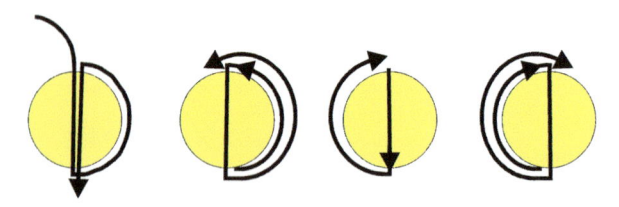

3. Stitch down through the head bead. Pick up the oval bead (body bead), one 3mm, one tube, one bicone and one 11/0 bead (turn bead). Skip the turn bead and stitch back up all the beads. Hold the turn bead and pull to adjust the tension. Pick up two 11/0 beads and stitch down through the head and body beads. Pick up one 3mm, one tube, one bicone and one 11/0 (turn bead). Skip the turn bead and stitch back up all the beads. Hold the turn bead and pull to adjust the tension. Stitch up through one of the top 11/0 beads and down the other. Repeat the thread path on each leg to reinforce and strengthen.

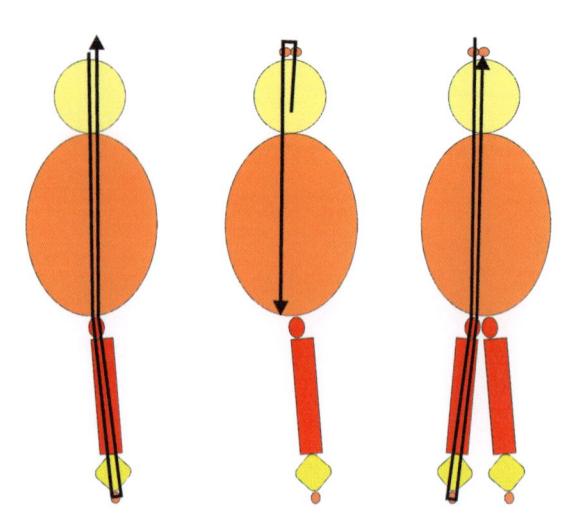

4. Pick up one 11/0, stitch under the wrapped thread and back up through the 11/0 bead (Brick Stitch). Repeat along the side of the head bead stopping near the body bead.

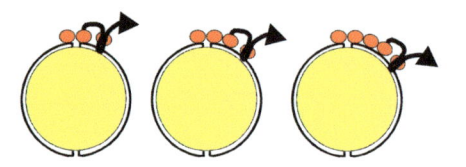

5. Create Kinky Fringe on the bottom bead traveling up to the center top according to the chart below. Read the notes on Kinky Fringe Shorthand page 53 to understand the chart. When you reach the last center bead on top, do not add the fringe into that bead yet. Instead repeat step 4 to add the brick stitch beads to the other side. Then repeat this step adding the fringe from the bottom to the top and complete the fringes into each brick stitch bead.

Fringe Chart: (From the bottom of the face to the top)
Bottom   5t, -2   (see illustration)
Next up   6t, -3
Next up   7t, -2,-3
Next up   8t, -2,-3
Next up   9t, -2,-3
Next up   10t, -3,-3 and repeat this on the remaining beads to the top

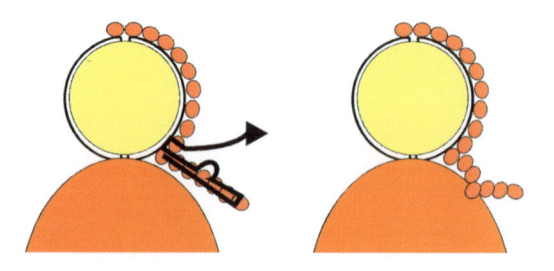

6. Knot the thread ends, weave in and cut.

7. Glue the pin finding to the back of the body bead.

Tip: The key to the design of this project is a large flat bead for the body so that you have an area to glue the pin back finding to. Then select a round bead for the head and use the tube beads for the legs. Shoe beads work great in this design or use any dice cut cube or diamond bicone for the feet. The instructions for creating the kinky fringe hair is the same as the project.

55

Project 2 – Kinky fringe

This project uses a different color bead at the kink spots on the fringe and shows how this design choice emphasizes the kink and introduces a spark of color into the fringe. This design has an equal number of beads between kinks, is the same in each fringe with a reduced count of total length of the fringe.

Supplies:

12 grams seed beads 11/0 red transparent
2 grams seed beads 11/0 bright copper metallic
2 grams bugle beads 7mm red opaque
1 gram seed beads 6/0 red transparent
30 each oval beads 8 x 10mm red transparent
30 each round beads 3mm copper metallic
1 each puffed rectangle bead 30x22mm clear/red/copper
Standard beading kit (page 92)
Standard necklace kit (page 92) gold

Steps:

1. Create a ladder with 20 columns of one red 11/0, one bugle, and one red 11/0 using the instructions for Basic 3-bead Ladder Stitch on page 88 and 2 yards of thread.

2. Create a ladder with 14 columns of one red 11/0, one bugle, and one red 11/0 using the instructions for Basic 3-bead Ladder Stitch on page 88 and 2 yards of thread. Repeat so you have two strips of 14 columns of ladder stitch.

Create the fringe:

In the next two steps, create the fringe using the respective fringe charts. In the charts "R" designates the red 11/0 beads, "C" is the copper 11/0 beads and "T" is the turn bead using a 11/0 copper bead. Stitch back up the strand creating a kink at each copper bead (skip each copper bead).

3. Cut 2 yards of thread and put a needle on to work with single thread. Add a stop bead with a six inch tail. Add fringe to one of the 14-column strips then repeat on the other 14-column strip. Use the chart below to create the fringe. Remove the stop bead, knot the thread, weave in and cut. Leave the needle thread for use later.

Fringe Chart:

Column	beads
1	3R,C,5R,C,5R,T
2	4R,C,5R,C,5R,T
3,4	5R,C,5R,C,5R,T
5-9	5R,C,5R,C,5R,C,5R,T
10-14	5R,C,5R,C,5R,C,5R,C,5R,T

4. Cut 3 yards of thread and put a needle on to work with single thread. Stitch up the 10th and down into the 11th column and pull until there is a 1 ½ yard tail. Wrap the tail in a sticky note for use later (Half thread method page 87). Add fringe to the 20-column strip using the chart below starting in the center and working to the edges. Knot, weave and cut the thread end.

Fringe Chart:

Column	beads
8 to 13	5R,C,5R,C,5R,C,5R,C,5R,C,5R,C,5R,T
7,14	3R,C,5R,C,5R,C,5R,C,5R,C,5R,C,5R,T
6,15	5R,C,5R,C,5R,C,5R,C,5R,C,5R,T
5,16	3R,C,5R,C,5R,C,5R,C,5R,C,5R,T
4,17	5R,C,5R,C,5R,C,5R,C,5R,T
3,18	3R,C,5R,C,5R,C,5R,C,5R,T
2,19	5R,C,5R,C,5R,C,5R,T
1,20	3R,C,5R,C,5R,C,5R,T

5. Use the needle thread from the 14-column strips to attach each of the 14 column strips (side strips attached at column 14) to the 20 column strip (bottom strip) using the thread path below. Repeat the thread path two more times to reinforce. Knot the thread, weave in and cut.

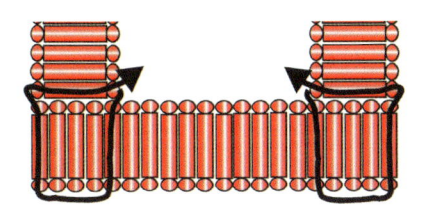

6. Cut 1 yard of thread and put a needle on to work single thread. Add a stop bead with a six inch tail. Stitch up the 10th column in the bottom strip and pick up the rectangle bead and one 6/0 bead. Stitch back down through the rectangle bead into the 11th column of the bottom strip. Hold the 6/0 bead like a turn bead and pull to adjust the tension. Repeat the thread path two more times to reinforce and strengthen. Remove the stop bead. Use the needle and tail thread to tie a square knot. Weave in the ends and cut.

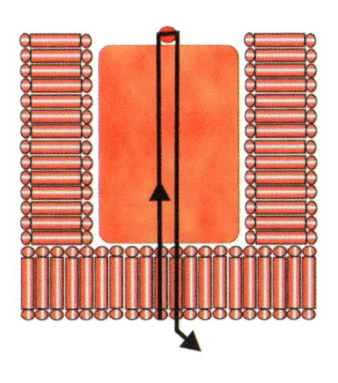

7. Cut 3 yards of thread and put a needle on. Move the needle to the middle to work with doubled thread. Use the instructions for Stringing with Thread on page 89. For the strand, pick up one 6/0. Then pick up one 3mm and one oval bead and repeat 14 times. Pick up one red 11/0 and stitch through the top of the side strip. Pick up six to eight red 11/0 beads adjusting as needed to fit from the side strip to the 6/0 bead on top of the rectangle. Stitch through the 6/0 bead and pick up six to eight red 11/0 beads and stitch through the top of the other side strip. Pick up the beads for the other side of the strand, matching the first in mirror image.

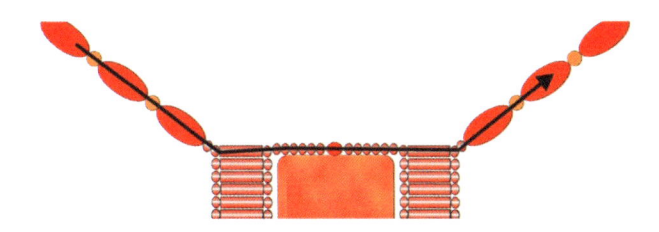

8. Finish with findings page 90.

57

Project 3 - Kinky Fringe

In this project, we'll use larger beads at the skip points in the fringe to create a sharper corner on the kink.

Supplies:

14 grams seed beads 11/0 crystal color lined mint
4 grams seed beads Delicas 8/0 light blue transparent matte
10 grams fringe beads (aka 4mm drop beads) medium blue transparent rainbow
10 grams fringe beads (aka 4mm drop beads) lime green transparent rainbow
10-11 each jelly roll disc beads 12mm jonquil/aqua AB
1 each slide clasp 3-hole silver
12 each jump rings 5mm silver
Standard beading kit (page 92)

Steps:

1. Create a ladder with 55 columns of 8/0 seed beads using the instructions for Basic 1-bead Ladder Stitch on page 88. Repeat for a total of two strips.

2. Cut three yards of thread and put a needle on. Move the needle to the center to work doubled thread. Add a stop bead with a 12 inch tail. Line the strips up. Stitch up the bottom strip, down the next column and up the third column. Pick up one disc and stitch through the corresponding column on the top strip. Stitch up and down the columns to the fifth column over. Pick up one disc and stitch through the corresponding column on the bottom strip. Repeat the pattern across the strips.

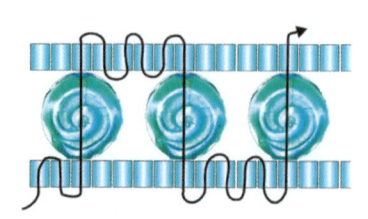

3. Pick up fifteen 11/0 beads and measure against the end of the bracelet (figure 1). Add or subtract beads until you have the number of beads equal to the distance plus one. Stitch through the column on the other strip (figure 2). Pick up eight or more 11/0 beads as needed to span the distance between the strips and stitch around the top loop (figure 3). Stitch through the first column, pick up three 11/0 beads, and stitch through the middle five beads on the loop. Pick up three 11/0 beads and stitch through the strip bead (figure 4). Repeat the thread path to reinforce (figure 5). Knot the thread, weave in and cut. Add needles on to the tail threads on the other end and repeat the step at that end.

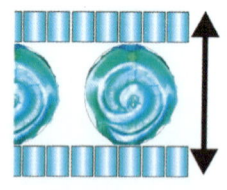

figure 1

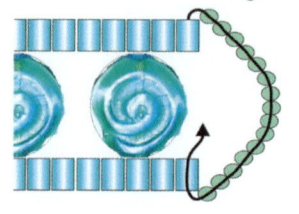

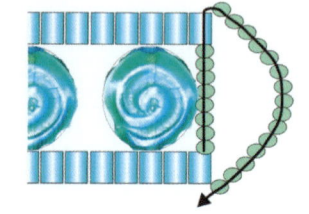

figure 2

figure 3

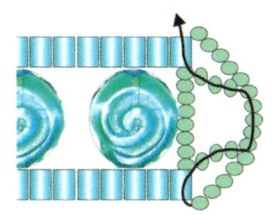

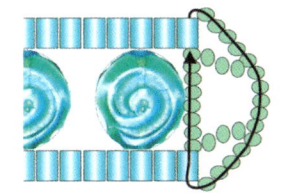

figure 4

figure 5

4. Add the Kinky fringe. Cut 2 yards of thread and put a needle on to work single thread. Stitch into the end strip bead and out the next pulling until there is a six inch tail. Use the needle and tail threads and tie a square knot plus (page 91). Weave in the tail thread and cut. Create fringes across the strip using the same design (below) for each fringe. Add new thread when the current thread is approximately six inches. When you reach the end of the bracelet, tie knots in the thread, weave in and cut. Repeat on the other side of the bracelet.

Fringe Chart:

Pick up three 11/0, one blue fringe bead, three 11/0, one blue fringe bead, three 11/0, one lime fringe bead, two 11/0 ending with a lime fringe bead as the turn bead.

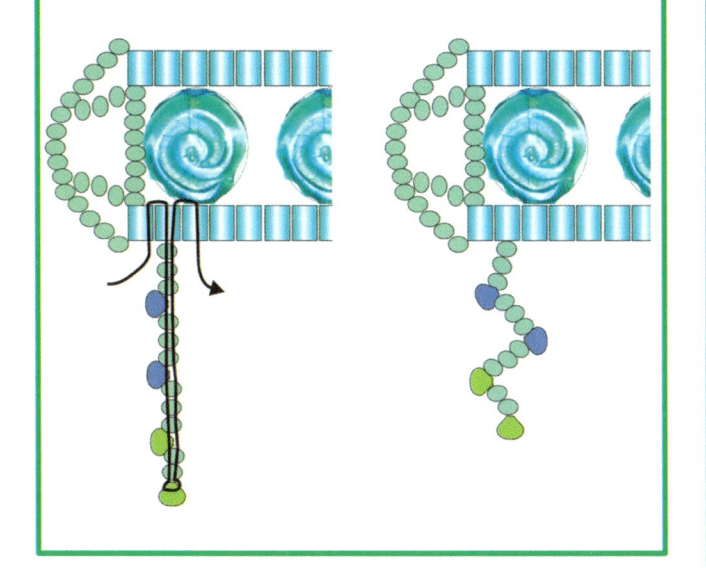

Adding thread-

Stop using the current thread (red in the figure below). Add a needle to two yards of thread and stitch up the previous column and down the current column with the new thread (purple in the figure below). Use the old needle and new tail and tie a square knot plus. Weave in the ends and cut. Continue with the new thread.

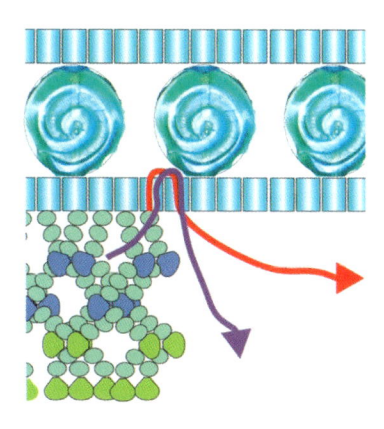

5. See Finish with Findings on page 90 and attach the clasp.

Tip: Tap into your creative juices and try other colors and use other shapes of beads in the center. And what could be more natural for a Kinky bracelet than spikes!

Chapter 6: Branch Fringe

Branch fringe is like a celebration of fringe since it essentially is fringe on a fringe strand! It is typically created using single thread. The variety of appearances that can be achieved with branch fringe is vast. Creating more branches produces thicker, fuller fringe. Short branches can look like spikes while longer branches hang lower from gravity. Branches can end simply with a seed bead or incorporate other beads. Branches can be added throughout the length of the fringe, or only in some areas. And, don't forget, branches can have branches! With all of these options, the variety of designs is endless with this type of fringe, but the construction techniques are the same.

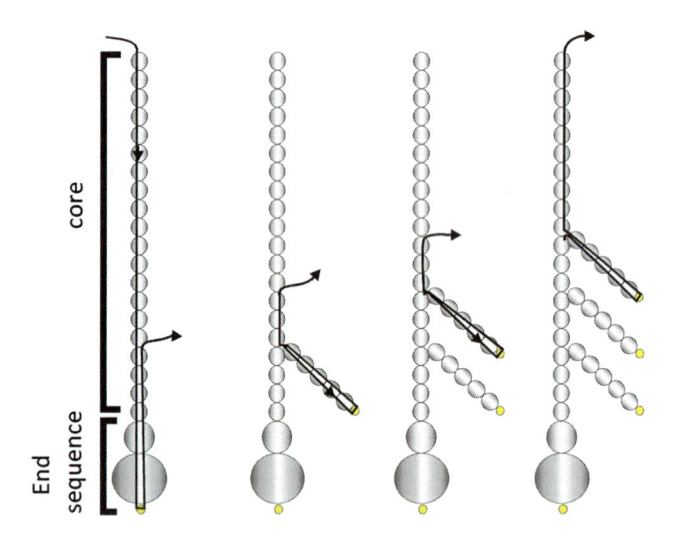

Steps

1. Exit the beadwork where you want to attach the fringe strand.

2. Pick up beads for the fringe strand (the core) plus an end sequence (optional) and a turn bead. Skip the turn bead and stitch up through beads into the core to the location for the first branch.

3. Hold the turn bead with one hand and pull on the thread with the other hand to adjust the tension. Pull the tension as tight as possible. The steps that follow will introduce ease into the strand, so start with as tight a tension as possible to avoid having to adjust it later.

4. Pick up beads for the branch plus a turn bead. Move the beads so they are next to the core. Stitch back through the branch beads skipping the turn bead, and stitch up into the core to the intersection of the next branch.

5. Pull the thread. When almost all of the thread is pulled through and there is a small loop left, reposition the branch making sure it is next to the core. Pull slightly on the thread near the branch to remove any excess thread and position the turn bead as illustrated. Now pull on the needle thread for the final tension. Do not pull tight, pull only enough to remove ease in the thread.
Branches create corners and pulling tightly will pull the corners straight and destroy the tension needed. If your design calls for the branch to hang down, position the branch like in figure 1. If, instead, you want the branch to stick out, position the branch like in figure 2.

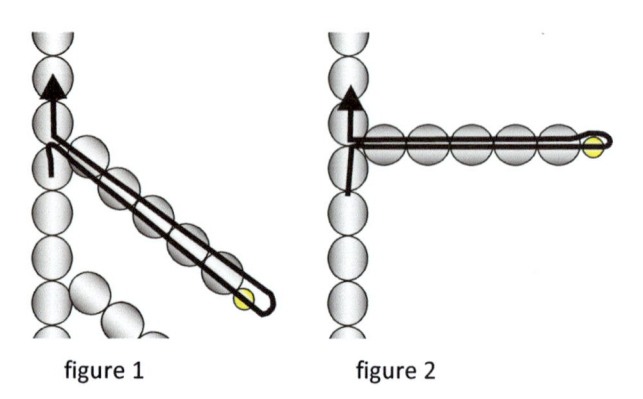

figure 1   figure 2

6. Repeat steps 4 and 5 for each branch and finally stitch up into the beadwork.

> Tip: If you find that you need to adjust the tension when you are in the middle of the fringe, return to the first branch, correct the tension there and then continue up to each next branch and adjust each in order one by one.

How to design Branch Fringe:

• Select the seed beads and any other beads you want to use in the fringe. Thread a needle with a 1/2 yard of thread and put on a stop bead. Use this to design your fringe. Key points to consider follow.

• The longer the branches, the fuller the fringe.

• More branches produces fuller fringe.

• Branches do not have to be the same size throughout.

• Heavier branches will hang straight down. Weight can be a result of the length of the branch and/or using beads larger (and heavier) than seed beads in the branch.

• Shorter, lighter branches will stick out more.

• The initial construction for branch fringe is a standard fringe so all of the design possibilities apply like end sequences and/or color variations.

• Branches can span the entire core, can be added to the end sections only, or anywhere in between.

• Branches are like fringes, so they can include beads other than seed beads. Each of the Fringe End designs (like picot, leaf or stars page 10) can be used on the core strand and/or the branch ends.

• Branches (and branches on branches) can be created with colors that are the same as the core or different colors. The branches can also use a different size beads in the branch than used in the core.

• Create your center, longest fringe. Write down the core count and the intervals to the branches and the branch sizes. Next, create the final fringe. Finally, decide a profile for the bottom (e.g. a 'v' shape, "U" shape, etc.) and count the number of fringes from the center to the side. Use all of this information to plan and calculate your decrease. Adjust as needed.

These branches are short and span the entire core.

These branches are long and are on the ends only.

Branches are short and positioned in the middle

Fringe, plus two branches using Leaf End.

The center fringe of this necklace is a core of 45 with an end sequence plus 2 branches. The last fringe on the side

62

is a core of 6 with one branch added. There are a total of 31 fringes, or 16 from center to end. This resulted in a plan as follows: The center and the next fringe on each side are created with a core of 45 to create a "U" shape. Then a decrease of two is used for the next two fringes. Finally a decrease of three is used for the remaining fringes. Two branches are added to all except the last two fringes on each side which are simply standard fringes.

- Branch fringe designs can be different from other fringes in the way gravity impacts how it hangs down. Other fringe designs are greatly impacted by gravity and will hang straight down. However, the fullness of branch fringes can provide a base of sorts so that the fringes on the side are held up by previous fringes and therefore may not hang straight down.

- Branches are essentially fringe strands on a fringe strand and typically are in the style of standard fringe. However, there are also Circle Branches (see below) or loops (right).

the same bead entering at the bottom of the bead. Continue stitching up the core to and through the next attachment bead.

Loop Branches:

Loop branches are created by stitching up to the attachment point between two core beads. Pick up one bead and then beads for the loop. Move the beads next to the core and stitch up the first added bead plus into the core entering at the attachment point. This type of fringe works best when the loop beads are smaller than the core beads. For instance, in Project 7 page 76, the core is 11/0 beads while the loop branches are 13/0 charlotte cut beads. In the project, the bottom center of the loop is a small fringe bead.

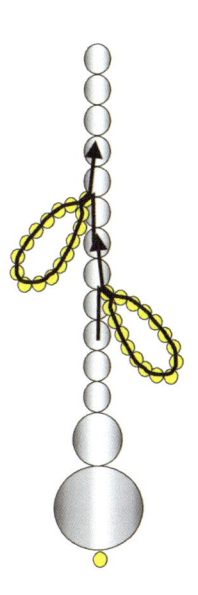

Circle Branches:

In the necklace above, the core is created with 11/0 beads and the circles are fifteen each 15/0 beads with alternating colors. Circles are created by stitching up the core to an attachment bead and stitching up through that bead. Pick up beads for the circle and stitch up through

- When you are designing and stitching fringe, it is helpful to take notes so that you can repeat the design again either on another piece or the other side of symmetrical fringe. Here is an easy to read and useful method for branch fringe.

Branch Fringe Shorthand:

20ET, -4, +5t -3, +4t -2, +3t

The first number is how many beads to pick up for the full strand (the core) plus an end sequence plus a turn bead. If there was no end sequence, you can note as simply "t". If you have more than one end sequence, designate each with a letter and use the appropriate letter in your notes. The subsequent numbers are the count of beads to stitch up the strand to reach the position to add a branch and how many beads are in the branch. After the last numbers, simply travel up the remaining beads in the core. So, this notation means pick up 20 beads, the end sequence plus a turn bead. Skip the turn bead stitch up the end sequence plus four beads up the core and add a branch that is five beads long plus a turn bead. Complete that branch and stitch up three beads into the core and add a branch that is four beads long plus a turn bead. Complete that branch and stitch up the core two beads and add a branch that is three beads long plus a turn bead. Complete that branch and stitch up the remainder of the core.

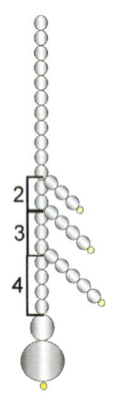

You can use an end sequence on some or all branches. If you are using multiple end sequences designate each with a letter and note as "eAt", "eBt", etc. If you are using different colors for your branches, these can also be designated with a letter code. For example if red is R, orange is G, and yellow is Y, then " R20ET, -4,+R5t -3, +G4t -2, +Y3t " means pick up twenty red for the core and the first branch is red, the next is orange and the last is yellow. When practiced, this code is easy to use and lets you document complicated designs concisely and accurately.

Another example is 20+es_pt, -8, +5Rt -6, +5t -4, +4t. This is a fringe with a count of 20 seed beads plus the end sequence with a picot style turn bead(20+es_pt) . The first branch is 8 seed beads up the core and is 5 beads long plus a 3mm round and a turn bead (-8+5Rt). The next branch is 6 beads up the core and is 5 beads long plus a turn bead. The last branch is 4 beads up the core and is 4 beads long plus a turn bead.

Use parentheses () to designate when there are branches on branches. See the project on page 72 for an example and illustrations.

64

Project 1 - Branch Fringe

Supplies:

60 grams 11/0 seed beads color lined aqua
8 grams bugle beads 6mm lime opaque
150 each Czech Fire polish beads 4mm aqua blue opal
Standard beading kit (page 92)
Standard necklace kit (page 92) silver

Steps:

Create the base structure -

1. Cut 3 yards of thread and put a needle on to work with single thread. Use the 11/0, bugle, and 4mm fire polish beads with the instructions for the 3-bead Ladder Stitch page 88 and Ladder stitch with windows page 89. Create the base section as illustrated below with 20 windows (21 bugle sections). Note that the window sections have one 11/0, one 4mm and one 11/0 on one side of the strip and two 11/0, one 4mm and two 11/0 on the other side of the strip.

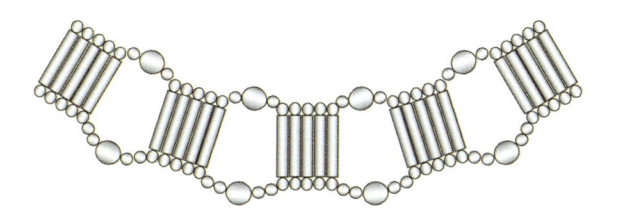

2. When you reach the end, create a loop. Pick up 11/0 seed beads equal to the length of the set of seed-bugle-set on the end plus one more bead (usually 6 to 8 beads) and stitch into the other side of the end set. Repeat the thread path three more times to reinforce.

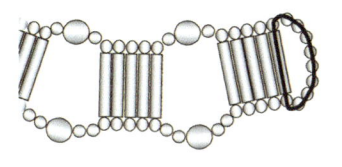

3. After creating the end loop above, stitch back through the entire base structure. When you reach starting end, create a loop using the previous step.

4. Use the tail and needle threads and tie a square plus knot. Weave in the ends and cut.

Create the fringe.

5. Cut 4 yards of thread. Wrap 2 yards up into a sticky note for use later (Half Thread Method page 87). Put a needle on the other end to work single thread. Add a stop bead near the sticky note. Start in the center section, noted as "A" in figure below. Stitch up through the second column, pick up one 11/0 and down through the third

column. Pull until the stop bead rests near the bottom of the second column. You are now positioned to do the center fringe on the center section, working from the center to the right.

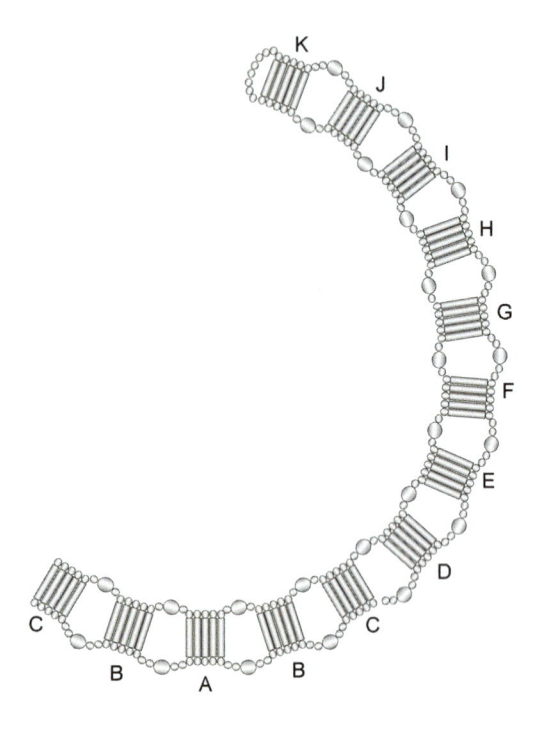

The end sequence is one 11/0 aqua, one bugle, one 11/0 aqua, one 4mm and a turn bead of one 11/0 aqua.

- When you stitch to the top of a column, pick up one 11/0, then stitch down to the next column, except when you reach the window. In that case, do not pick up a bead, simply travel through the 11/0, 4mm, 11/0 in the window and down the column to the next section.

- Use a core of 30 for each of the fringes in section "A", using Style 1.

- For the sections noted "B", start with a core count of 30 and reduce by one for the subsequent fringes. Use Style 1 until you get to a core count of 26 (the last fringe in the section) and switch to Style 2.

- For the sections noted "C", start with a core count of 26 and reduce by one for the subsequent fringes. Use Style 2.

- For the section noted "D", start with a core count of 22 and reduce by one for the subsequent fringes. Use Style 2 except at a core count of 20 and fewer, stop adding the top branch of 4.

- For section "E", start with a core count of 18 and reduce by one until you reach a core of 15. The fringes with a core count of 18, 17 and 16 use Style 2 without the top branch of 4. The final two fringes in this section use a core of 15 and Style 3.

- Complete the remaining sections (F through K) using a core count of 15 with Style 3.

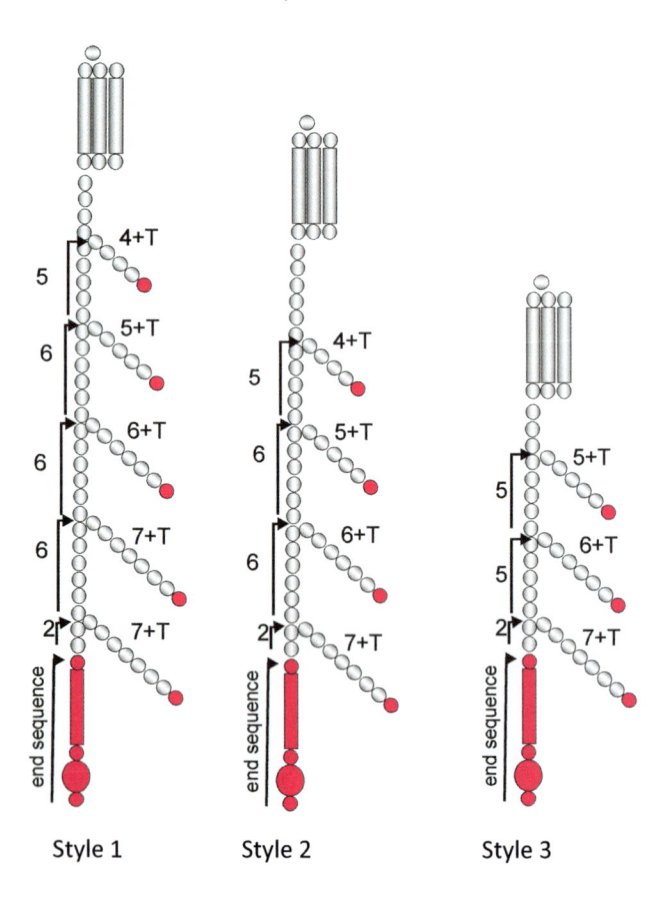

Style 1   Style 2   Style 3

Style 1: Pick up the count for the core plus the end sequence. Stitch back up through the end sequence plus 2 beads on the core. Add a branch of 7 beads plus a turn bead. Travel 6 beads up the core. Add a branch of 7 beads plus a turn bead. Travel 6 beads up the core. Add a branch of 6 beads plus a turn bead. Travel 6 beads up the core. Add a branch of 5 beads plus a turn bead. Travel 5 beads up the core. Add a branch of 4 beads plus a turn bead. Travel the remaining distance up the core to finish.

Style 2: Pick up the count for the core plus the end sequence. Stitch back up through the end sequence plus 2 beads on the core. Add a branch of 7 beads plus a turn bead. Travel 6 beads up the core. Add a branch of 6 beads plus a turn bead. Travel 6 beads up the core. Add a branch of 5 beads plus a turn bead. Travel 5 beads up the core. Add a branch of 4 beads plus a turn bead. Travel the remaining distance up the core to finish.

Style 3: Pick up the count for the core plus the end sequence. Stitch back up through the end sequence plus 2 beads on the core. Add a branch of 7 beads plus a turn bead. Travel 5 beads up the core. Add a branch of 6 beads plus a turn bead. Travel 5 beads up the core. Add a branch of 5 beads plus a turn bead. Travel the remaining distance up the core to finish.

Alternate Fringe Chart (Fringe shorthand page 64)
(Column count from center out to end)

Section	column	Fringe
A	All	30ESt, -2 +7t, -6 +7t, -6 +6t, -6 +5t, -5 +4t
B	1	30ESt, -2 +7t, -6 +7t, -6 +6t, -6 +5t, -5 +4t
	2	29ESt, -2 +7t, -6 +7t, -6 +6t, -6 +5t, -5 +4t
	3	28ESt, -2 +7t, -6 +7t, -6 +6t, -6 +5t, -5 +4t
	4	27ESt, -2 +7t, -6 +7t, -6 +6t, -6 +5t,- 5 +4t
	5	26ESt, -2 +7t, -6 +6t, -6 +5t, -5 +4t
C	1	26ESt, -2 +7t, -6 +6t, -6 +5t, -5 +4t
	2	25ESt, -2 +7t, -6 +6t, -6 +5t, -5 +4t
	3	24ESt, -2 +7t, -6 +6t, -6 +5t, -5 +4t
	4	23ESt, -2 +7t, -6 +6t, -6 +5t, -5 +4t
	5	22ESt, -2 +7t, -6 +6t, -6 +5t, -5 +4t
D	1	22ESt, -2 +7t, -6 +6t, -6 +5t, -5 +4t
	2	21ESt, -2 +7t, -6 +6t, -6 +5t, -5 +4t
	3	20ESt, -2 +7t, -6 +6t, -6 +5t
	4	19ESt, -2 +7t, -6 +6t, -6 +5t
	5	18ESt, -2 +7t, -6 +6t, -6 +5t
E	1	18ESt, -2 +7t, -6 +6t, -6 +5t
	2	17ESt, -2 +7t, -6 +6t, -6 +5t
	3	16ESt, -2 +7t, -6 +6t, -6 +5t
	4,5	5ESt, -2 +7t, -5 +6t, -5 +5t
F-K	all	15ESt, -2 +7t, -5 +6t, -5 +5t

6. When you finish all fringes to the right, tie a knot, weave in the thread and cut.

7. Remove the thread from the sticky note and remove the stop bead. Add a needle to the thread and use it to complete the fringes to the left using the steps above.

8. Use two jump rings and attach the hook to one end loop. Use two jump rings and attach the chain to the other end. Put beads on the headpin. Use wire cutters to trim the head pin and pliers to loop it on the end of the chain.

Tip: Adding thread while stitching fringe.
Add thread as follows. First, end the current thread by stitching down into the next column. Cut a new piece of thread and put a needle on. With the new thread, stitch up from the previous column and down into the next column leaving a 5 inch tail. Use the tail and needle thread and tie a square knot plus (page 91). Weave the ends in and cut. Continue with the new thread.

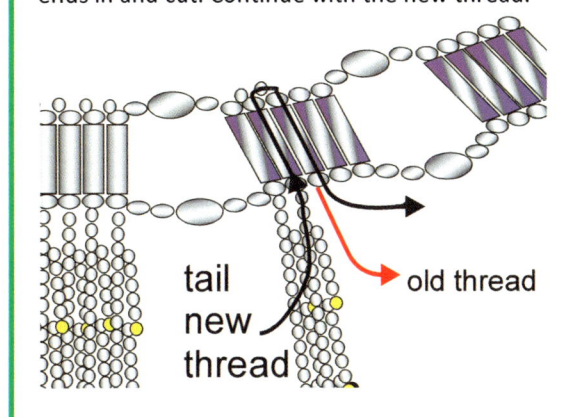

Project 2 – Branch Fringe

Not ready for a full blown collar project? This fabulous bib style necklace is based on the previous project but takes much less time (and beads!) to complete, but still has the "wow" factor.

Supplies:

20 grams 11/0 seed beads navy metallic
2 grams 11/0 seed beads gold metallic
3 grams twisted bugle beads 6mm navy metallic
36 ea Czech Fire polish beads 4mm navy metallic
35 ea. glass beads 6mm window cut round navy metallic
Standard beading kit (page 92)
Standard necklace kit (page 92) gold

Steps:

1. Use the 11/0, bugle, and 4mm fire polish beads with the instructions for the 3-bead Ladder Stitch page 88 and Ladder stitch with windows page 89 using 2 yards of thread. Create the base section as illustrated below with four windows and five bugle sections. Note that the window sections have one gold 11/0, one 4mm and one gold 11/0 beads on one side of the strip and two gold 11/0, one 4mm and two gold 11/0 beads on the other side of the strip. The 3-bead columns use the blue 11/0 beads.

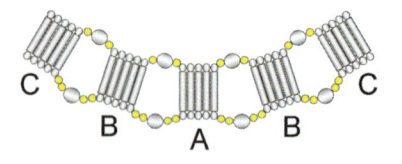

2. Cut 4 yards of thread. Wrap 2 yards up into a sticky note for use later (Half Thread Method page 87). Put a needle on the other end to work single thread. Add a stop bead near the sticky note. Start in the center section, noted as "A" in figure above. Stitch up through the second column, pick up one 11/0 blue and down through the third column. Pull until the stop bead rests near the bottom of the second column. You are now positioned to do the center fringe on the center section, working from the center to the right.

• The end sequence is one 11/0 gold, one bugle, one 11/0 gold, one 4mm and a 11/0 gold for the turn bead.

• When you stitch to the top of a column, pick up one 11/0 blue, then stitch down to the next column, except when you reach the window. In that case, do not pick up a bead, simply travel through the seed, 4mm, seed in the window and down the column to the next section.

• Use a core of 30 for each of the fringes in section A, using Style 1 page 66.

• For the sections noted "B", start with a core count of 30 and reduce by one for the subsequent fringes. Use Style 1 until you get to a core count of 26 (the last fringe in the section) and switch to Style 2 page 66.

• For the sections noted "C", start with a core count of 26 and reduce by one for the subsequent fringes. Use Style 2 page 66.

Alternate Fringe Chart (Fringe shorthand page 64)
(Column count from center out to end)

Section	column	Fringe
A	All	30ESt, -2 +7t, -6 +7t, -6 +6t, -6 +5t, -5 +4t
B	1	30ESt, -2 +7t, -6 +7t, -6 +6t, -6 +5t, -5 +4t
	2	29ESt, -2 +7t, -6 +7t, -6 +6t, -6 +5t, -5 +4t
	3	28ESt, -2 +7t, -6 +7t, -6 +6t, -6 +5t, -5 +4t
	4	27ESt, -2 +7t, -6 +7t, -6 +6t, -6 +5t,- 5 +4t
	5	26ESt, -2 +7t, -6 +6t, -6 +5t, -5 +4t
C	1	26ESt, -2 +7t, -6 +6t, -6 +5t, -5 +4t
	2	25ESt, -2 +7t, -6 +6t, -6 +5t, -5 +4t
	3	24ESt, -2 +7t, -6 +6t, -6 +5t, -5 +4t
	4	23ESt, -2 +7t, -6 +6t, -6 +5t, -5 +4t
	5	22ESt, -2 +7t, -6 +6t, -6 +5t, -5 +4t

3. When you finish all fringes to the right, tie a knot, weave in the thread and cut.

4. Remove the thread from the sticky note and remove the stop bead. Add a needle to the thread and use it to complete the fringes to the left, using steps 12 through 15.

Add the necklace strands:

5. Use the chart below with the 6mm round and gold 11/0 beads and instructions for the Necklace Strand with Side Attachment on page 89 and create the necklace strands.

Project 3-Branch Fringe

This project includes short branches that span the entire core and have different end sequences.

Supplies:

17 grams 11/0 seed beads olive transparent
3 grams 11/0 seed beads gold metallic
1 gram 15/0 seed beads olive transparent
15 each leaf bead top drilled 10 x 17mm crystal vitrail
34 each flat rectangle beads 8 x 11 mm olive transparent
40 each Czech fire polish beads 4mm watermelon foil
20 each Czech fire polish beads 6mm olive transparent
1 each puffed oval cloisonné bead 30 x 24mm gold/pink/green
18 inches flexible beading wire .019
2 each 2-hole connectors
Standard beading kit (page 92)
Standard necklace kit (page 92) gold plus 8 more jump rings

Steps:

Create the base -

1. Create a ladder with 31 columns of two olive 11/0 seed beads using the instructions for Basic 2-bead Ladder Stitch on page 99.

Create the fringe -

2. Cut 6 yards of thread and put on a stop bead with a 3 yard tail to use the Half-thread Method (page 87).

3. Start in the center (the 16th column). After creating the fringe for a column add one seed bead before stitching down to the next column for the next fringe. Create the fringe using the Fringe chart below. When the fringes are finished on one side, knot the thread, weave in and cut. Put a needle on the tail thread and repeat on the other side.

There are two different end sequences.

End Sequence R

One gold 11/0, one 4mm and one gold 11/0 turn bead.

End Sequence L

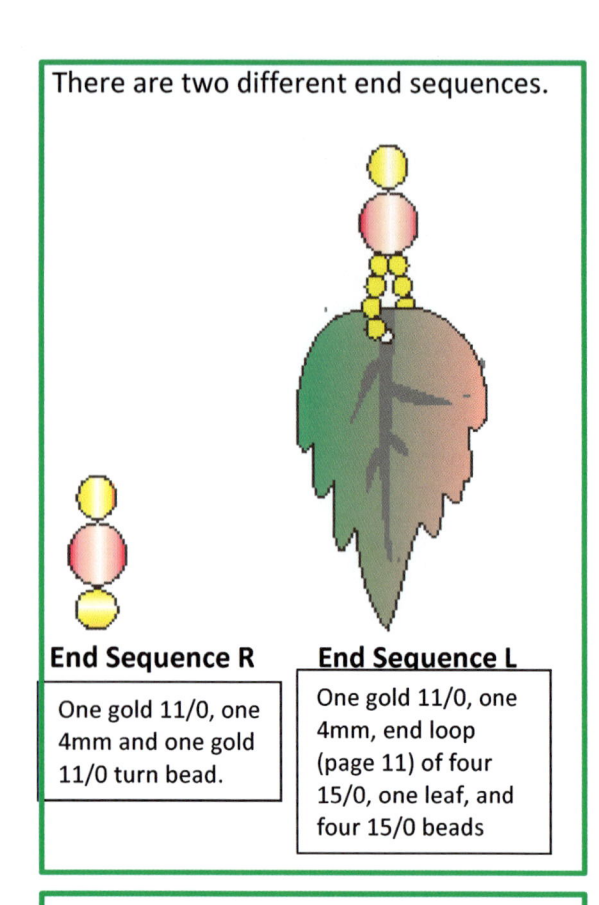

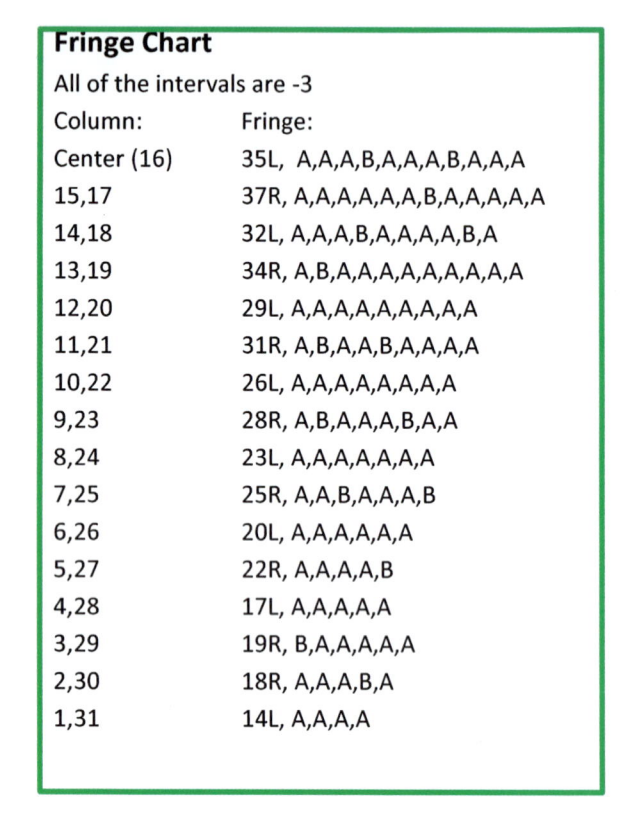

One gold 11/0, one 4mm, end loop (page 11) of four 15/0, one leaf, and four 15/0 beads

There are two different branch styles:

Style A

Three olive 11/0 and one gold 11/0 turn bead.

Style B

One olive 11/0, one 4mm and one gold 11/0 turn bead.

Samples: Columns 2,10 and 1,31

Fringe Chart

All of the intervals are -3

Column:	Fringe:
Center (16)	35L, A,A,A,B,A,A,A,B,A,A,A
15,17	37R, A,A,A,A,A,B,A,A,A,A,A
14,18	32L, A,A,B,A,A,A,A,B,A
13,19	34R, A,B,A,A,A,A,A,A,A,A
12,20	29L, A,A,A,A,A,A,A,A,A
11,21	31R, A,B,A,A,B,A,A,A,A
10,22	26L, A,A,A,A,A,A,A,A
9,23	28R, A,B,A,A,A,B,A,A
8,24	23L, A,A,A,A,A,A,A
7,25	25R, A,A,B,A,A,A,B
6,26	20L, A,A,A,A,A,A
5,27	22R, A,A,A,A,B
4,28	17L, A,A,A,A,A
3,29	19R, B,A,A,A,A,A
2,30	18R, A,A,A,B,A
1,31	14L, A,A,A,A

Add the necklace strands:

4. Use figure 1 below with the rectangle and gold 11/0 beads and instructions for Necklace Strand with Side Attachment on page 89 and create the necklace strands.

5. Use figure 2 below with the flexible beading wire and the rectangle, 4mm and 6mm fire polish, gold 11/0, and the cloisonné beads with the instructions for Stringing with Flexible Beading Wire page 89 to create the other necklace strand.

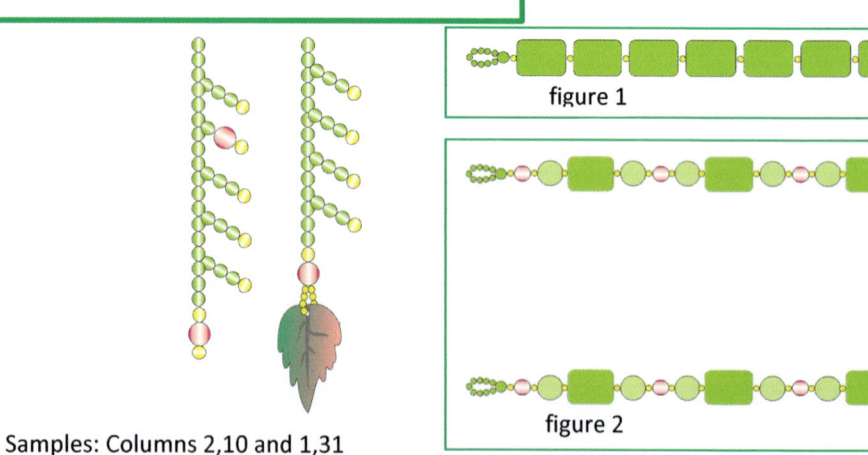

figure 1

figure 2

70

Project 4 – Branch Fringe

This branch fringe design includes an "end sequence" of beads with long branches below the sequence.

Supplies:

13 grams 11/0 seed beads purple transparent (color X)
3 grams 11/0 seed beads blue clr-lined rainbow (color A)
3 grams 11/0 seed beads purple matte (color B)
3 grams 11/0 seed beads periwinkle blue opaque (color C)
3 grams 11/0 seed beads blue color-lined (color D)
1 gram 11/0 seed beads metallic dark gold
39 each round bead 4mm metallic dark gold
62 each round bead 6mm gold speckled tanzanite
26 each metal rondelle 4x1mm antique gold
12 each round tube bead 6 x 10mm tanzanite transparent
1 metal leaf drop 63 x 30mm antique gold
18 inches flexible beading wire .019
2 each 2-hole connectors
Standard beading kit (page 92)
Standard necklace kit (page 92) gold plus 9 extra jump rings

Steps:

Create the base -
1. Create a ladder with 31 columns of two color A seed beads using the instructions for Basic 2-bead Ladder Stitch on page 88.

Create the fringe -
2. Cut 6 yards of thread and put on a stop bead with a 3 yard tail to use the Half-thread Method (page 87).
3. Start in the center (the 16th column). After creating the fringe for a column add one seed bead before stitching down to the next column for the next fringe. Create the fringe using the Fringe chart below. When the fringes are finished on one side, knot the thread, weave in and cut. Put a needle on the tail thread and repeat on the other side.

This fringe design has some 4mm beads in the core with the 11/0 beads all in color X. The use and placement of the 4mm beads are designated as "*" in the fringe chart. The branches are varying colors, noted as A, B, C or D. Each branch is ten (10) beads plus a turn bead. The turn beads match the beads used in the core or branch.

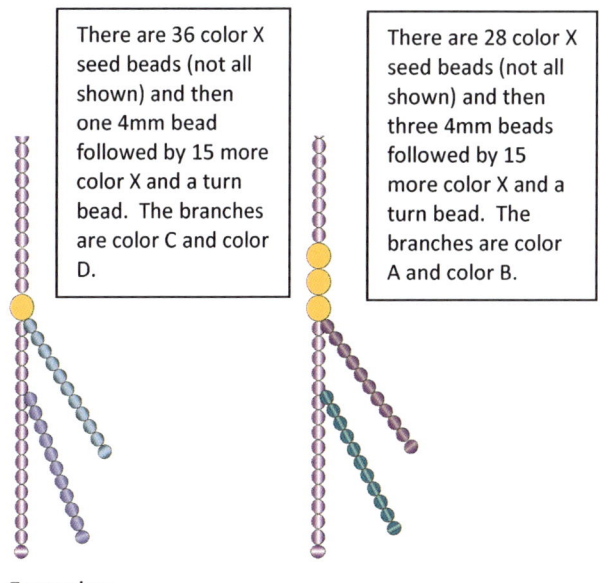

| There are 36 color X seed beads (not all shown) and then one 4mm bead followed by 15 more color X and a turn bead. The branches are color C and color D. | There are 28 color X seed beads (not all shown) and then three 4mm beads followed by 15 more color X and a turn bead. The branches are color A and color B. |

Examples:
column 9,23   column 8,24

Fringe Chart (each branch is 10 beads plus a turn bead)

Column	core	branches
Center	50 * 15t	-10 +A, -5 +B
15,17	48 * 15t	-10 +C, -5 +D
14,18	46 * 15t	-10 +A, -5 +B
13,19	44 * 15t	-10 +C, -5 +D
12,20	42 * 15t	-10 +A, -5 +B
11,21	40 * 15t	-10 +C, -5 +D
10,22	38 * 15t	-10 +A, -5 +B
9,23	36 * 15t	-10 +C, -5 +D
8,24	28 *** 15t	-10 +A, -5 +B
7,25	18 ***22t	-10 +C, -5 +D, -7 +A
6,26	11 ***27t	-10 +D, -5 +A, -5 +B, -7 +C
5,27	3 *** 32t	-10 +A, -5 +B, -5 +C, -5 +D, -7 +A
4,28	41t	-10 +B, -5 +C, -5 +D, -5 +A, -5 +B, -5 +C, -5 +D
3,29	39t	-10 +C, -5 +D, -5 +A, -5 +B, -5 +C, -5 +D
2,30	36t	-10 +A, -5 +B, -5 +C, -5 +D, -5 +A, -5 +B
1,31	33t	-10 +A, -5 +B, -5 +C, -5 +D, -5 +A

Project 5 – Branch Fringe:

This project includes branches created on branches for a full fun fringe.

Add the necklace strands:

4. Use figure 1 below with the 6mm round, rondelle, tube and gold 11/0 beads and instructions for the Necklace Strand with Side Attachment on page 89 and create the necklace strands.

5. Use figure 2 below with the flexible beading wire and the 6mm round and gold 11/0 beads with the instructions for Stringing with Flexible Beading Wire on page 89 to create the other necklace strand. After you construct the necklace strand, use a jump ring and attach the leaf drop to the center.

Supplies:

8 grams 11/0 seed beads amber transparent
1 gram 15/0 seed beads bright gold metallic
88 each fire polish beads 3mm crystal AB
2 each round hollow glass beads 14mm amber/white/gold
4 each metal bead caps 8mm (optional)
2 each ear wires fish hook style gold
Standard beading kit (page 92)

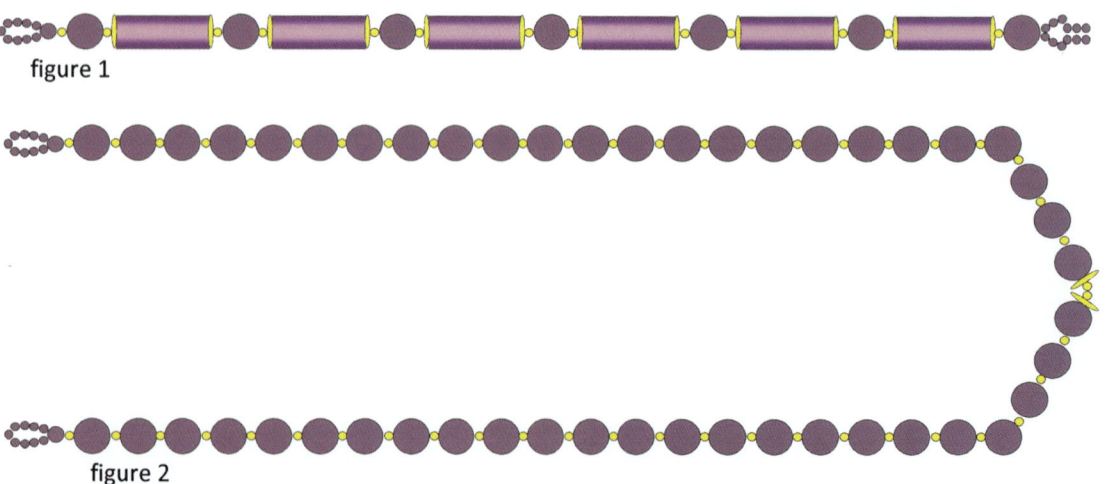

figure 1

figure 2

Steps:

1. Create a ladder with 3 columns of amber 11/0 beads using the instructions for Basic 2-bead Ladder Stitch on page 88 except use 3 yards of thread and do not weave in and cut the thread ends. Continue using the needle thread, position the tail thread and knot on the bottom of the strip.

2. Stitch up the first column and down the second (middle) column. Create the center fringe according to the fringe chart (Figure 1). Stitch down the third column and create the fringe there (figure 2). Pick up eight 11/0 seed beads and stitch down the first column (figure 3). Create the fringe on the first column (figure 4). Stitch through the top loop to the third column and back again to reinforce as illustrated in figure 5.

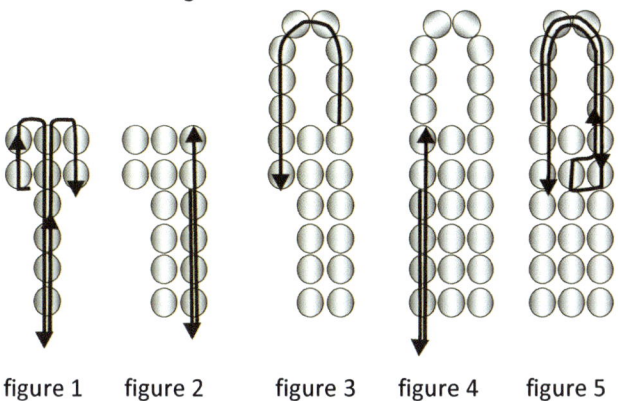

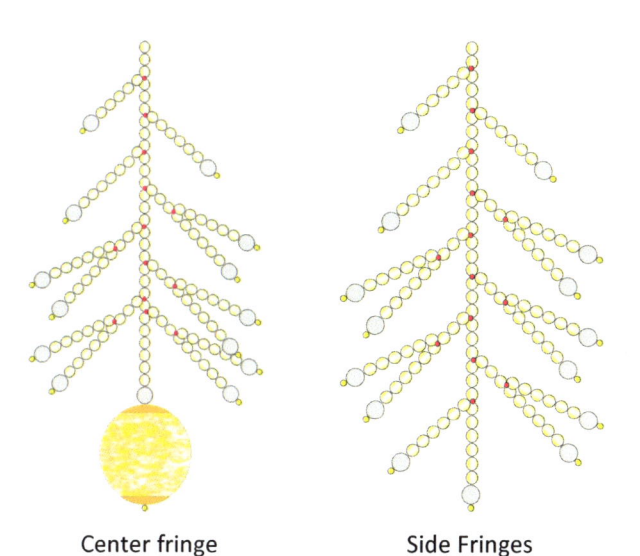

figure 1   figure 2   figure 3   figure 4   figure 5

Center fringe   Side Fringes

3. Use the needle and tail thread and tie a square knot. Weave in the ends and cut.

4. Repeat all steps for the second earring. For each earring, use the pliers to twist open the loop on the ear wires, insert the beaded loop, then close.

Fringe chart using shorthand:

Column

1, 3   32T   -6 +6 -3, (+9 -6 +6) -3, (+9 -6 +6) -3, (+9 - 6 +6) -3, (+9 -6 +6) -3, (+9 -6 +6) -3, +7 -3, +6 -3, +5

2   28ET   -6, (+9 -6 +6) -1, (+9 -6 +6) -3, (+9 -6 +6) -3, (+9 -6 +6) -3, +7 -3, +6 -3, +5

T= 3mm plus 15/0 seed bead (turn bead) AND use on each of the branches
ET=3mm, bead cap, 14mm, bead cap, three 1/15 picot end

Tip: Experiment with other shapes for the bottom blown glass bead, and changing seed bead colors on some branches.

73

Project 6 – Branch Fringe

Branches can be positioned at each and every intersection of beads in the core. When laying down flat, this resembles a feather, but when hung and worn (influenced by gravity), it is a full rich fringe. In fact it is so full, that just one fringe creates a great look for the stick pin in this project.

Supplies:
2 grams 11/0 seed beads blue opaque luster (color A)
3 grams 11/0 seed beads blue opaque matte (color B)
1 gram 11/0 seed beads pink ceylon
1 gram 15/0 seed beads bright gold metallic
1 each cloisonné bead puffed square diagonal corner drilled blue with pink design
1 each stick pin 2 1/2 inch with loop and clutch gold
2 each jump rings 5mm gold
Standard beading kit (page 92)

Steps:

1. Cut 3 yards of thread and put a needle on to work single thread. Pick up nine color A and move down the thread leaving a 6 inch tail. Stitch through the beads again and pull to create a loop. Use the needle and tail threads and tie a square knot. Stitch around the loop again to reinforce.

2. Create the fringe. The End Sequence is the same at the end of the fringe for each branch and consists of one 11/0 pink and one gold (turn bead). For the fringe, pick up the 14mm bead and 55 color A beads plus the end sequence and stitch up three beads into the core. The first branch uses Color A and is 3 beads plus the end sequence, then travel one bead up the core. Each branch is positioned up the core one (1). For subsequent branches increase the number of beads in the branch by one until the count reaches 12. When the count is 12 switch to Color B for the branches. Continue to add branches up the core one bead, using color B and a count of 12 plus the end sequence until there are seven beads left in the core, noted in red in figure X. Continue adding branches up the core one bead but reduce the count by one for each subsequent branch until the count is seven. Finish with a count of seven. Stitch up the 14mm bead. Use the tail and needle threads and tie a square knot. Weave in the ends and cut.

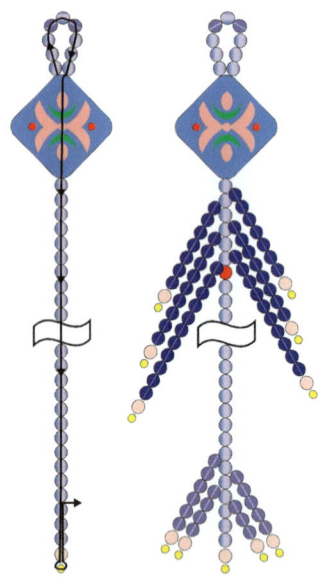

4. Use pliers and the jump rings to attach the top beaded loop to the stick pin loop. Use two jump rings.

Project 7– Branch Fringe:

This project introduces the Loop branch style of branch fringe. (page 63)

Supplies:

13 grams 11/0 seed beads cobalt transparent
1 gram 11/0 seed beads gold metallic
17 grams 13/0 charlotte cut seed beads dark blue AB (approx. 1 ½ hanks)
2 grams 15/0 seed beads gold metallic
8 grams small fringe beads cobalt rainbow
33 each Czech fire polish beads 4mm dark blue AB
31 each dagger beads 15 x 6 mm light cobalt transparent
6 each round beads 6mm light cobalt transparent
28 each flat rectangle beads 8 x 12mm light cobalt
1 each cloisonné bead flat oval 15 x20 mm pink flowers on blue background]
Standard beading kit (page 92)
Standard necklace kit (page 92) gold

Steps:

Create the base -

1. Create a ladder with 31 columns of cobalt seed beads using the instructions for Basic 2-bead Ladder Stitch on page 88.

Create the fringe -

2. Cut 6 yards of thread and put on a stop bead with a 3 yard tail to use the Half-thread Method (page 87).

3. Start in the center (the 16th column). After creating the fringe for a column add one seed bead before stitching down to the next column for the next fringe. Create the fringe using the Fringe chart below. When the fringes are finished on one side, knot the thread, weave in and cut. Put a needle on the tail thread and repeat on the other side.

Fringe Chart:
- The fringe core is created with 11/0 cobalt beads plus the end sequence below.
- The center core is 45 with a decrease of 1 for each subsequent fringe.
- Each fringe has six loops with an interval of -5

End Sequence

The end sequence is the same for each fringe.

11/0 core beads

One 4mm fire polish

Four 13/0 beads, one dagger and four 13/0 beads (loop end page 11)

75

Loop Design

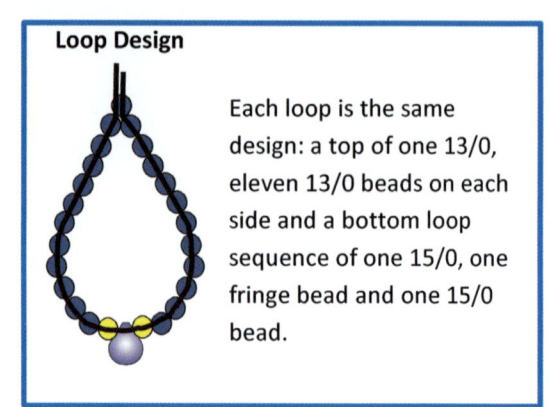

Each loop is the same design: a top of one 13/0, eleven 13/0 beads on each side and a bottom loop sequence of one 15/0, one fringe bead and one 15/0 bead.

4. Use figure 1 below with the rectangle and gold 11/0 beads and instructions for Necklace Strand with Side Attachment on page 89 and create the necklace strands.

5. Cut 2 yards of thread and put a needle on. Move the needle to the center to work with doubled thread. Stitch around the loop on the left side of the necklace strand. Pull until there is a 6 inch tail. Use the needle and tail threads and tie a square knot. Stitch through the necklace strand to the attachment area for the fringe section. Pick up five 13/0, one 4mm, one gold 11/0, one 6mm, one gold 11/0, one 6mm, one gold 11/0, one 6mm, one gold 11/0. Pick up the oval cloisonné bead and the previous beads in reverse order. Stitch through the other necklace strand past the 6/0 bead and before the loop. Cut the thread near the needle creating two threads, a needle and a tail. Use the needle thread and stitch around the loop. Pull both thread ends to adjust the tension and then tie a square knot. Stitch down the strand two inches with the needle thread. Put a needle on the tail thread. Stitch around the loop and then down the strand two inches. Cut the thread ends. Put needles on the thread ends on the left side, stitch each down the strand two inches and cut. (figure 2)

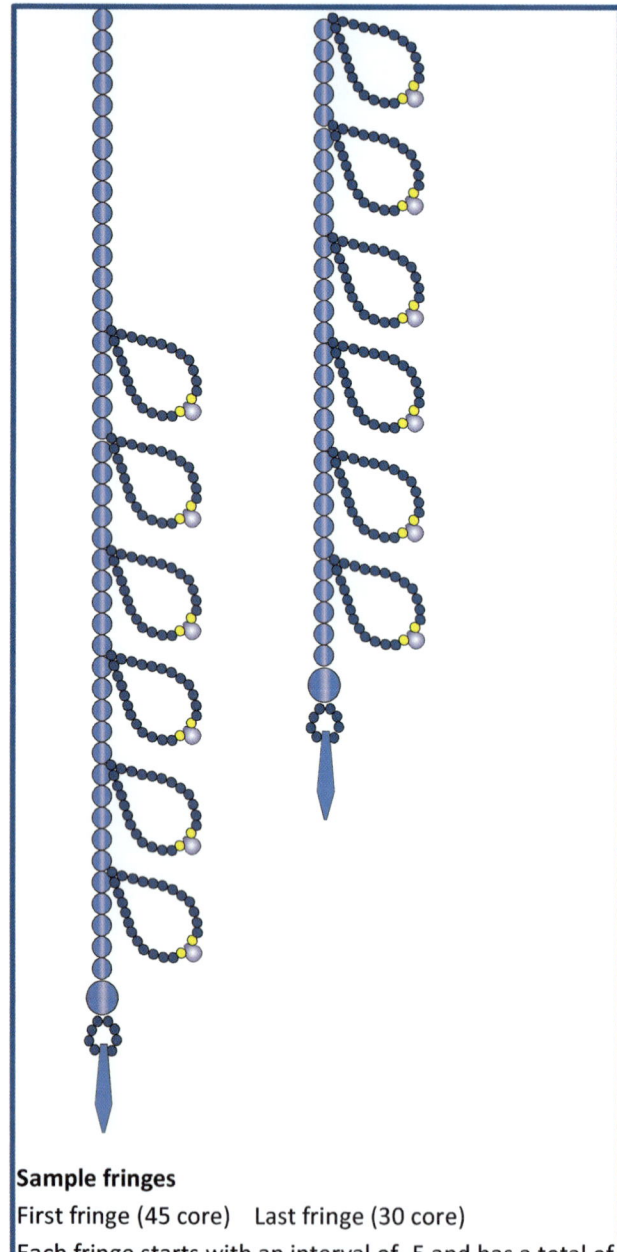

Sample fringes
First fringe (45 core)   Last fringe (30 core)
Each fringe starts with an interval of -5 and has a total of six loop fringes, all with an interval of -5

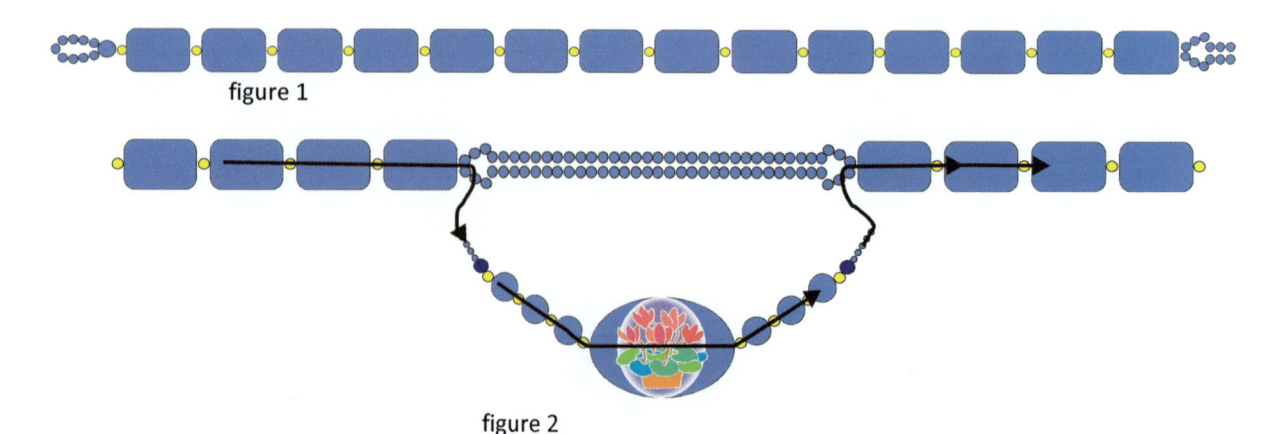

figure 1

figure 2

Chapter 7: Twisted and Spiral Fringes

Twists and turns and spinning spirals are a fun way to add dimension into fringe designs. The instructions that follow detail how to create these fabulous fringes.

How to create Twisted Fringe:

Twisted fringe is a variation of loop fringe. If you are not careful when you create Loop Fringe and allow some twist in your thread, then you may notice the loops turn a little and do not fall the same as the other loops. Twisted Fringe capitalizes on that phenomenon to create a gracefully fun fringe design. Like Loop Fringe, Twisted fringe is created with doubled thread and works best when you have two connection points into the beadwork.

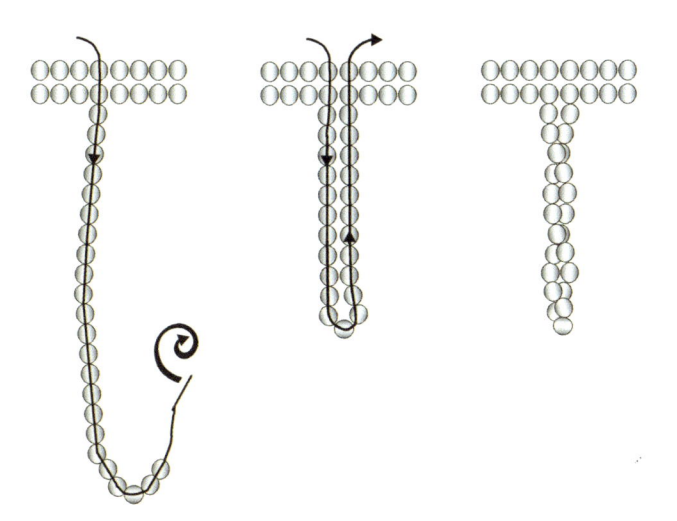

Steps:

1. Exit the beadwork where you want to attach the fringe strand. Pick up seed beads for the fringe. This will typically be a long strand since it is both sides of the loop.

2. Move the beads up to the beadwork.

3. Hold the needle between your thumb and index finger. Rub together, pushing your thumb forward, index finger backward and rolling the needle between them and making the needle twist. Reposition the needle to the center again and perform the roll again. Repeat one more time for a total of three roll sequences.

4. Near the needle, insert a straight pin, your finger or a pencil between the two threads. Gently push the pin/finger/pencil between the two threads toward the beads, moving the twist in the thread to the inside of the fringe strand.

5. Set something heavy on the thread near the beads to keep the twist inside the beads. Repeat steps 3 and 4. For a tighter twist, repeat steps 4 and 5 again.

6. Pinch the thread near the beads keeping the twist inside the strand and stitch up into the beadwork with the other hand. Pull to adjust the tension, finally releasing the pinch. The tension should be firm but not tight. When you lift the beadwork from the surface, the fringe will naturally twist.

Variation:- Twisted top with end sequence beads:

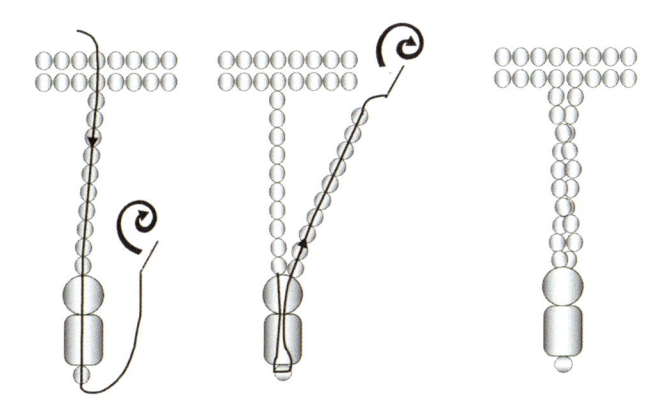

Steps:

1. Exit the beadwork where you want to attach the fringe strand. Pick up the seed beads for one side plus the end sequence and turn bead.

2. Do steps 2 through 5 on page 77. Since this is only half the thread fewer finger rolls are needed.

3. Pinch the thread near the bead strand to hold the twist inside. Use your other hand and stitch up the end sequence, skipping the turn bead. Pull to tighten and release the pinch. The turn bead should be flush into the end bead. Be sure to pull the thread tight to hold the turn bead tight into the end bead so the thread is pinched and will hold the twist already done.

4. Pick up the seed beads for the other side.

5. Do steps 2 through 6 on page 77.

> **Tip:** Twisted fringe can be created with single thread. The resulting fringe will look different since the doubled thread fills the bead holes more and therefore makes the individual strands look smoother. If using single thread, you will need to perform the roll many more times. With single thread, there is no way to move the twist into just the beaded area, so the entire thread must be twisted. In order to control the twist between fringe strands and achieve consistency, it is recommended that you not only count your rolls, but also untwist the thread before starting each new fringe.

How to design Twisted Fringe:

• Select the seed and other beads you may want to use in the fringe.

• Decide whether you want to create with seed beads alone or with an end sequence.

• Using doubled thread, create your center/longest fringe on the beadwork using the applicable steps above. Write down the number of seed beads used and the number of finger rolls. Pick up the beadwork with the fringe attached to test the length and how much twist was achieved. Undo and adjust as desired.

> **Tip:** With other types of fringe, it is easier to create a test strand using a short piece of thread. However, Twisted Fringed needs to be stitched into beadwork to hold the twist in the thread. So, it is often easier to test and create the fringe design right on the beadwork.

• Plan your decrease. Use another needle and doubled thread with a stop bead and create the last fringe on one side. Note the count of beads and number of finger rolls used. Pick up the beadwork with the fringe attached to test the length and how much twist was achieved. Looking at the center and last fringe, decide if your plan gives you the desired results or make adjustments as needed. Remove the last fringe created in this step (done as a test only), then return to the center and finish creating your fringe.

• Twisted fringe designs can be seed beads only, or a bead sequence on the bottom as noted above.

• Note that the width (thickness) of Twisted Fringe is two beads wide. It is best when there are two connection points since this will provide adequate spacing between fringe strands.

• Each side of the twist can be the same color or, you can emphasize the twist by using one color for half of the beads (half of the "loop") and a different color for the other side.

• You can also shade colors down the strand by picking up different colors down the loop then picking up in reverse sequence up the other side of the loop.

Project 1 – Twisted Fringe

This project includes regular Twisted Fringe and the variation with an end sequence. Some twisted strands are one color, others twist two colors. This use of color provides shading across the fringe strands.

Supplies:
2 grams 11/0 seed beads yellow transparent rainbow (color A)
2 grams 11/0 seed beads dark yellow opaque luster (color B)
2 grams 11/0 seed beads tangerine transparent luster , (color C)
2 grams 11/0 seed beads dark orange color lined luster (color D)
2 grams 11/0 seed beads light siam transparent AB (color E)
2 grams 11/0 seed beads red color lined (color F)
2 grams 11/0 seed beads dark red rainbow (color G)
2 grams 11/0 seed beads maroon color lined (color H)
2 grams 11/0 seed beads garnet transparent (color I)
(or select nine colors of seed beads from light to dark)
8 each round beads 4mm dark gold metallic
4 each round tube beads 4 x10mm dark gold metallic
4 each diamond bicone beads 5mm dark gold metallic
46 each round faceted beads 6mm sun yellow opaque
70 each round faceted beads 4mm orange opaque
1 each butterfly pendant 60 x 45mm gold and yellow enamel
2 each 2-hole connectors antique gold
Standard beading kit (page 92)
Standard necklace kit (page 92) gold plus 4 more jump rings

Steps:
Create the base -
1. Create a ladder with 28 columns of seed beads using the instructions for Basic 2-bead Ladder Stitch on page 88 with the pattern in the Base Chart below.

Create the fringe -
2. Cut 6 yards of thread. Put a needle on each end and move each of them 1 ½ yards (1/4 of the total yardage) from the ends to work with doubled thread using the Half Thread Method (page 87). Stitch down in the 14th column from the left and pull until there is 6 inches left on the short end of the thread. Use the other needle and stitch down the 13th column again pulling until there is 6 inches left on the short end of the thread. Reposition the needles as needed. Use the two short ends and tie a square knot. Weave in the ends and cut. Wrap the thread to the left in a sticky note and set aside to use later.

3. Start in the center (the 14th column) and working to the right. Create the fringe using the Fringe chart below. When the fringes are finished on one side, knot the thread, weave in and cut. Unwrap the other needle and finish the fringes to the left.

Base Chart:

A A A B B B C C C D D D E E E F F F G G G H H H I I I

Fringe Chart:

Column:	color	approx. count	length	color	approx. count	length
14,15	E	90	5 1/2 inches			
16,17	E	45	2 3/4 inches	F	45	2 3/4 inches
18,19	F	90	5 1/2 inches			
20,21	F	45	2 3/4 inches	G	45	2 3/4 inches
22,23	G	45	2 3/4 inches	H	45	2 3/4 inches
24,25	H	45	2 3/4 inches	I	45	2 3/4 inches
(the next fringe is Twisted Fringe with an end sequence variation)						
26,27	I	22	1 1/4 inches+ES	I	22	1 1/4 inches
28	I	10	standard fringe with end sequence			
13,12	E	45	2 3/4 inches	D	45	2 3/4 inches
11,10	D	45	2 3/4 inches	D	45	2 3/4 inches
9,8	D	45	2 3/4 inches	C	45	2 3/4 inches
7,6	C	45	2 3/4 inches	B	45	2 3/4 inches
5,4	B	45	2 3/4 inches	A	45	2 3/4 inches
(the next fringe is Twisted Fringe with an end sequence variation)						
3,2	A	22	1 1/4 inches+ES	A	22	1 1/4 inches
1	A	10	standard fringe with end sequence			

Note: This project calls for different colors of seed beads and not all seed beads are the same length. (See page 5). The length can vary from one color to another so that a count of 45 beads of one color is much longer or shorter than 45 beads of another color. The larger the count number, the more the difference can be exaggerated. So, in this project, instead of counting beads, use a ruler to measure the length of the strand. Start with the approximate count then measure and add or subtract as needed.

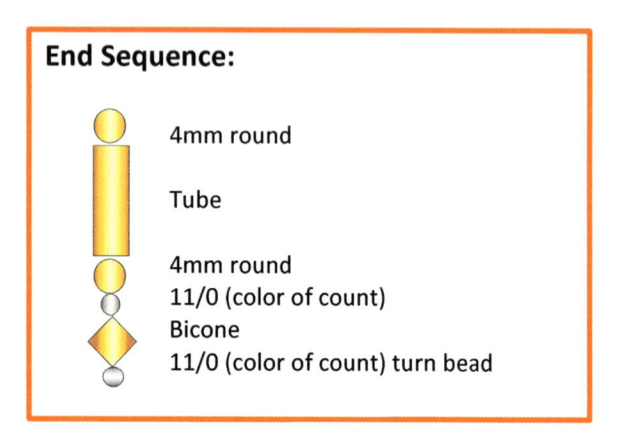

End Sequence:

4mm round
Tube
4mm round
11/0 (color of count)
Bicone
11/0 (color of count) turn bead

4. Use the chart below with the 6mm yellow and color B 11/0 beads and instructions for Necklace Strand with Side Attachment on page 89 and create the necklace strands.

5. Use the instructions for the Necklace Strand with Side Attachment on page 89 with the following exceptions. Create the strand with thirty five 4mm faceted beads. At step 2, instead of stitching through the bead base, pick up nine color C beads and create a loop around one of the attachment loops on the butterfly. Continue with the basic instructions to finish.

Spiral Fringe:

Spiral fringe is a technique of embellishing standard fringe and is created with single thread.

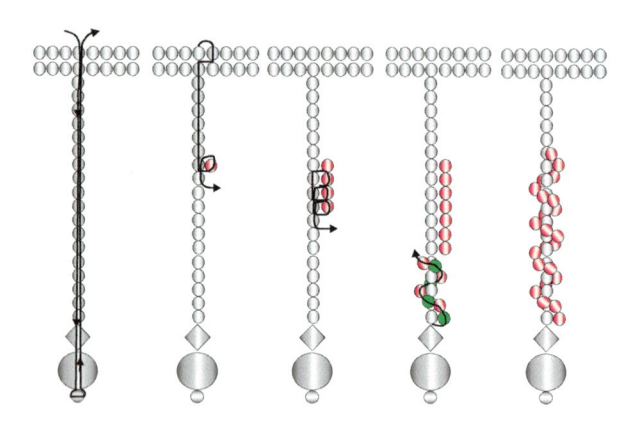

Steps:

1. Exit the beadwork where you want to attach the fringe strand.

2. Pick up seed beads, an end sequence if desired plus a turn bead. Move the beads up to the beadwork and stitch back up through the strand skipping the turn bead and into the beadwork just like Standard Fringe. Hold the turn bead with one hand and pull on the needle/thread with the other hand.

3. Stitch back down into the fringe strand positioning the needle two beads below the planned top of the spiral.

4. Pick up one seed bead and stitch around the seed bead in the strand and down one more bead. These are referred to as the spiral beads in the remaining steps.

5. Repeat step 6 until positioned at the bottom of the planned spiral.

6. Pick up one seed bead and stitch through the spiral bead above it. Continue picking up one bead then stitching though the next spiral bead all the way up the strand pushing the beads around the strand to look like a spiral repeating until reaching the last spiral bead. Pick up one more seed bead and stitch into and up through the strand to the beadwork.

7. If desired, you can smooth out the spiral by stitching through it again. On step 6 instead of stitching through the strand to the beadwork, stitch back into the spiral. Stitch around through the spiral beads down to the bottom of the spiral and into the bead strand. Either stitch up the bead strand to the beadwork or through the spiral beads again to the top of the spiral and then through the strand up to the beadwork.

How to design Spiral Fringe:

- Select the seed and other beads you may want to use in the fringe. Use a 1/2 yard thread with a stop bead and create the center/longest fringe. Write down the count of beads used. The core of the spiral is a standard fringe so review page 16 about how to design of standard fringe. Decide where you want the spiral and create.

- Use the same color beads for the spiral or a different color(s) from the core.

- Use a solid color core and shade the spiral using a different color seed bead from dark to light or vice versa

- Spirals can cover all or any part of the core. Spiral the entire length, just the bottom, just the top, or any selected area in the middle.

- Use a separate needle/thread and create the last fringe on one side, recording the counts. Use these fringes (middle and end) to evaluate your design, determine the spacing and placement of fringes on the beadwork and the lengths of the core sequences for the planned fringes in between. Make adjustments as desired.

- The width of the area with a spiral is three beads wide. In order to highlight the spiral, make sure there is enough spacing in between the fringes.

Project 2 – Spiral Fringe

This project includes Spiral fringe and Standard Fringe. The spiral bead colors are different than the core and coordinate with the end sequence of that fringe.

Supplies:

5 grams 11/0 seed beads lime opaque matte
2 grams 11/0 seed beads red opaque
2 grams 11/0 seed beads yellow opaque
2 grams 11/0 seed beads orange opaque
2 grams 11/0 seed beads dark green opaque matte
3 grams cube beads 3.5 to 3.7mm, green opaque rainbow matte
1 each lampwork glass bead red pepper 12 x 13mm
2 each lampwork glass beads pineapple 12 x 20mm
2 each lampwork glass beads orange with leaves 13 x 13mm
2 each lampwork glass beads green apple 12 x 12mm
8 each Czech glass leaf bead center drilled 10 x 13mm
7 each round beads 4mm yellow opaque
7 each round millefiori beads 6mm green/yellow/white
7 each metal rondelle beads 4 x 1 mm bright gold
Standard beading kit (page 92)
Standard necklace kit (page 92) gold

Steps:

Create the base -
1. Create a ladder with 35 columns of lime 11/0 beads using the instructions for Basic 2-bead Ladder Stitch on page 88.

Create the fringe -
2. Cut 6 yards of thread and put on a stop bead with a 3 yard tail to use the Half-thread Method page 87. Start in the center (the 18th column). After creating the fringe pick up one seed bead and stitch down the next column. Pick up one seed bead and stitch back up the column. Repeat adding beads above and under the columns moving to the next column for fringe placement. When the fringes are finished on one side, knot the thread, weave in and cut. Put a needle on the tail thread and repeat on the other side.

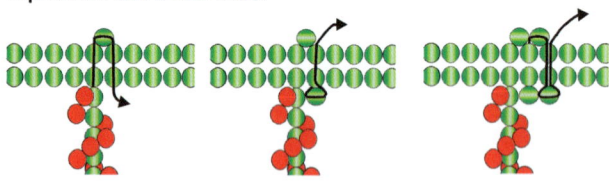

Fringe Chart:

Column	core count	end Bead	color of spiral	count down to spiral
18 (center)	45	pepper	red	1
22, 14	38	pineapple	yellow	6
26, 10	35	orange	orange	11
30, 6	28	apple	dark green	16
33, 3	see below			

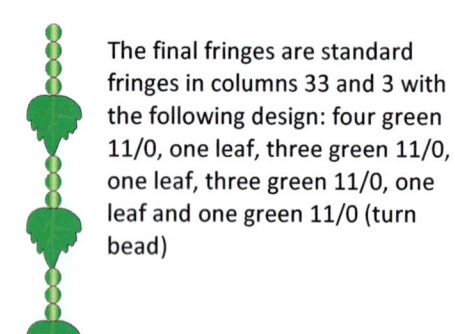

The final fringes are standard fringes in columns 33 and 3 with the following design: four green 11/0, one leaf, three green 11/0, one leaf, three green 11/0, one leaf and one green 11/0 (turn bead)

Add the necklace strands:
3. Cut 3 yards of thread and put a needle on to work single thread. Use the green 11/0 and cube beads to create the necklace strand starting with the instructions for the Basic 2-bead Ladder Stitch page 88 and then the Ladder Stitch with windows page 89. Leave a 1 yard tail and wrap in a sticky note. Use the pattern below and create a strand with sixteen windows ending at a window.

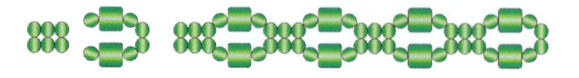

4. Attach to the fringed strip by stitching through the last column of the strip, then the previous column in the window and back to the last column as illustrated. Stitch through the next column in the strip, then back to the last column of the strip and then the column in the window. Stitch back through the entire strip to the start as in step 5 page 88.

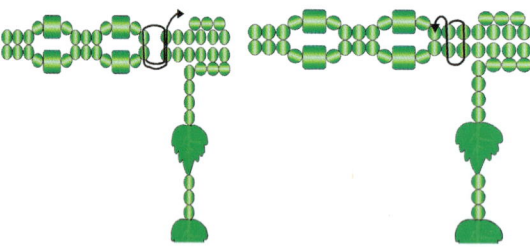

5. Pick up nine green 11/0 beads and stitch around the last column to create an end loop. Repeat the stitch path twice more to strengthen and reinforce. Use the needle and tail thread and tie a square knot. Use the needle thread and stitch around the loop one more time, weave into the columns and cut.

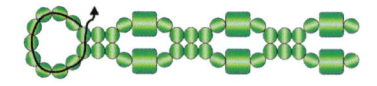

6. Unwrap the tail thread from the sticky note and put a needle on to work single thread. Add short fringes with a leaf end (page 11) to the center column between the windows and beads above as illustrated. On the last section before the fringed strip, do a standard fringe five green 11/0, one leaf bead and a green 11/0 bead (turn bead). Stitch over to the fringed strip and add beads to the top of the columns. Knot the thread, weave in and cut.

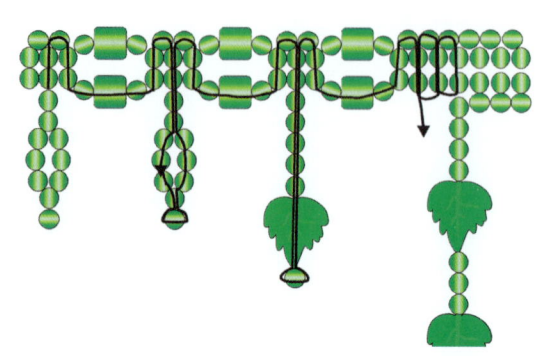

7. Repeat steps 3 to 6 on the other end of the necklace. Review Finish with Findings on page 90 and use the jump rings (two in each loop) and attach the hook to one side and the chain to the other.

Ribbon Spiral Fringe:

Ribbon Spiral Fringe provides a dramatic spiral, wider than the Spiral Fringe on page 80 and is created with single thread.

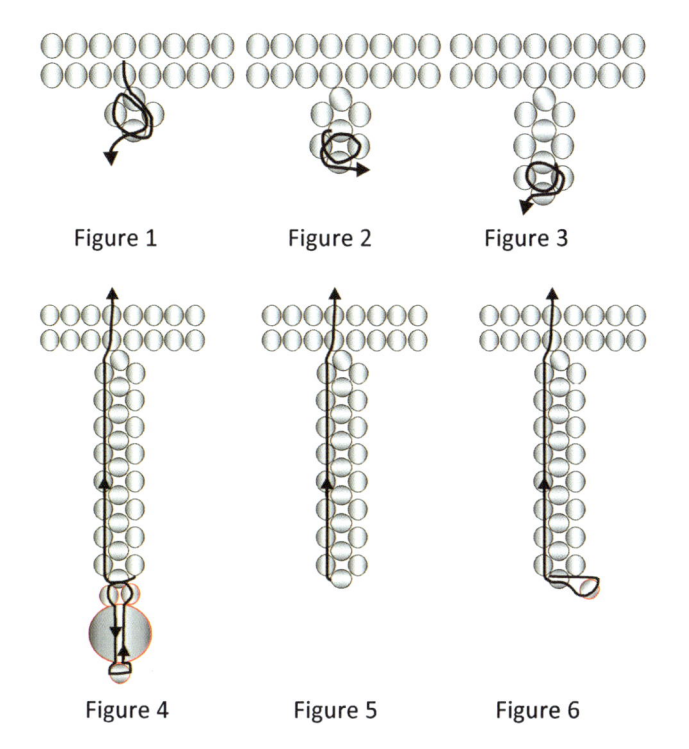

Figure 1

Figure 2

Figure 3

Figure 4

Figure 5

Figure 6

Steps:

1. Exit the beadwork where you want to attach the fringe strand.

2. Pick up four seed beads and move to position next to the beadwork. Stitch through the first three added beads again creating a circle (Figure 1).

3. Pick up three seed beads. Stitch through the top bead, entering the other side from where the thread is exiting. Pull to create a circle. Continue stitching around the circle two more beads to the bottom. (This is a strip of Right Angle Weave). Figures 2 and 3.

4. Repeat step 3 until you have the desired length. Approximately 5 1/2 inches of this stitch will result in approximately 2 1/2 inches of finished spiral. If you look at the construction of this fringe, you'll notice that the core of the spiral is one side of the Right Angle Weave. So, another method to estimate the final length is to string 11/0 beads until you have the length you desire. Count the number of beads used and construct a Right Angle Weave with a count on the side to match. While not exact, this will provide a good estimate.

5. On the last circle section, stitch around the beads again. If adding an end sequence, pick up the end sequence beads plus a turn bead. Stitch back through the end sequence skipping the turn bead and pull to adjust the tension (Figure 4). If not adding an end sequence, if the thread is exiting to the left it is in proper position for the next step (Figure 5). If the thread is exiting to the right, pick up a bead (use the same color as the center column if using multi colors) and stitch back through the bead to position the thread to exit the left side (Figure 6).

6. Stitch up through the left side beads all the way up the strand. Pull the thread twisting the beadwork into a spiral as you pull. Pull to a tight tension. Stitch up into the beadwork.

Smooth-it Option: The steps above create a standard Ribbon Spiral Fringe. This option adds beads to the outside edge of the spiral making it smooth. Stitch back down into the fringe on the outside edge of the spiral. Pick up one, two, or three beads as needed to fill in and stitch through the next outside bead. Repeat this down the spiral to fill in. Don't worry if some spaces may need 2 and others 3, the count does not have to be the same all of the way. Simply fill in as needed to create a smooth edge. Stitch all the way to the bottom and through the last bead there. Stitch back up through the outside edge beads to the top and finally into the beadwork.

Designing Ribbon Spiral Fringe:

• Select the seed and other beads you may want to use in the fringe. Use a 1 yard thread with a stop bead and create the center/longest fringe. Write down the count of 3-bead sections added by counting the number of beads on one side. Add the end sequence if desired and finish the fringe using the steps above.

• The ribbon can be created all in one color, or selecting a color for the core, another near the core and another for the outside edge.

• The ribbon can be the entire length of the fringe or any part of it

• The fringe can be designed with an end sequence or plain.

• Use a separate needle/thread and create the last fringe on one side, recording the counts. Use these to evaluate your design. Make adjustments as desired.

• This fringe is wide, approximately six beads wide. While you can create a bunched-up, chunky look by placing the spirals close together, if you provide adequate space, it will highlight the spirals within the fringe.

Project 3 – Ribbon Spiral Fringe

This project shows how to use three colors to shade the color of the core out to the edge to emphasize the shape. It uses both the standard process plus the Smooth It option.

Supplies:
3 grams 11/0 seed beads bright gold metallic
3 grams 11/0 seed beads cream ceylon
2 grams 11/0 seed beads light gold color lined
25 each round pearl beads 8mm cream
38 each round pearl beads 6mm cream
12 each round pearl beads 4mm cream
Standard beading kit (page 92)
Standard necklace kit (page 92) gold

Steps:
Create the base -
1. Use the metallic 11/0 beads and 4mm round beads to create the base with the instructions for Basic 2-bead Ladder Stitch on page 88 and the Ladder stitch with Windows page 89. Use the pattern below

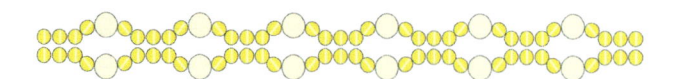

Create the fringe -
2. Cut 6 yards of thread and put on a stop bead with a 3 yard tail to use the Half-thread Method page 87. Start in the center. After creating the fringe pick up one seed bead and stitch down the next column. Stitch around under the window to the next section. Pick up one metallic 11/0 and stitch down into the center column for the next fringe. When the fringes are finished on one side, knot the thread, weave in and cut. Put a needle on the tail thread and repeat on the other side.

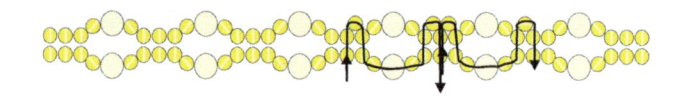

Fringe chart:
Use the below to show the placement spots for the fringe. The numbers are the counts of the side beads.

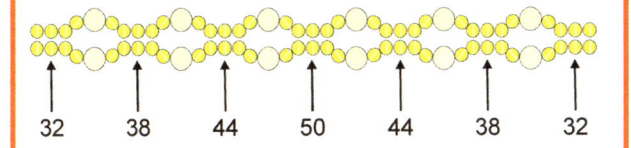

32 38 44 50 44 38 32

Start with one color lined, one cream, one color lined and one metallic 11/0 beads. Continue adding to the counts above with the metallic on the left, the color lined in the middle and the cream on the right. Add one 8mm pearl at the bottom and stitch up the left side through the metallic beads as the center core.

On the fringes with the counts of 32 and 44, stitch through again using the Smooth it option.

Add the necklace strand
3. Use the chart below with the 6mm and 8mm pearls and metallic 11/0 beads and instructions for the Necklace Strand with Side Attachment on page 89 and create the necklace strands. Use the cream ceylon 11/0 beads for the end loops.

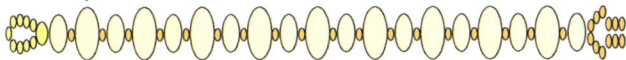

Project 4 - Ribbon Twist Fringe

Supplies:
2 grams 11/0 seed beads blue color lined pink (Color A)
3 grams 11/0 seed beads aqua color lined blue (Color B)
2 grams 11/0 seed beads cobalt transparent (Color C)
1 gram 6/0 4mm cube seed beads cobalt opaque
2 each ear wires fish hook style silver
Standard beading kit (page 92)

Steps:
1. Create a ladder with three columns of cobalt cube beads using the instructions for Basic 2-bead Ladder Stitch on page 88. Use 3 yards single thread and leave the tail thread for later use. Continue using the needle thread.

2. Position the strip so that the knot is on the top. Stitch down into the center column. Pick up one cube, and fifteen color A. Pick up one color B, one Color C, one color B and one color A for the first four beads and follow the instructions for creating Ribbon Twist Fringe with 20 sections. Stitch up the strand and pick up one color C. Stitch back down the strand and do the Smooth It Option on the twist filling in with Color C beads. After stitching up the strand, stitch down the last (third) column.

85

3. Create a fringe with thirteen color A and twenty right angle weave sections using the same color placement as in Step 2. Stitch up the strip, pick up eight color C beads and stitch down the first column. Create a fringe the same as in the third column and stitch up into the strip. Stitch through the eight-bead loop and down the third column. Stitch down to the twist and add the Smooth It Option filling in with color C beads. Stitch up through the strip, across the eight-bead loop and repeat the Smooth It Option on the first column. Stitch up through the strip. Use the needle and tail threads and tie a square knot. Weave in the ends and cut

4. Repeat all steps for the second earring. For each earring, use the pliers to twist open the loop on the ear wires, insert the beaded loop, then close.

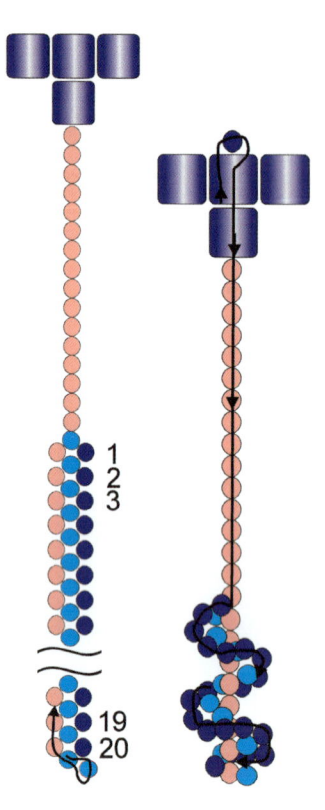

Tip: The most frequent error in constructing fringe is forgetting to include a bead in the strand. To help prevent this, make piles of each bead in the strand in the same order as it is used in the strand. If a bead is used twice then make two piles (see olive below). This will make creating the strand easier and faster. Once you have picked up all the beads and moved to the beadwork, pause to look at the strand compared to the previous strand. Check to see the current strand includes all of the beads and are in the proper order. Check also that the length of the strand is as desired.

Tip: Often the strand is longer than the needle. Stitch up the strand just short of the length of the needle. Pull ONLY to create a small loop so that you have enough room to insert the needle again. Repeat until you reach the top of the fringe. Now pull the needle thread to eliminate the small loops. Then perform the final pull for the whole strand.

Chapter 8: Basic Procedures

Basic Procedures:

Culling beads

It is necessary to cull seed beads as you bead. Culling is the process where you eliminate certain beads and don't use them. Typically, culling is performed by critically looking at each bead as you pick it up to use it. If a bead is not shaped properly or very short or very long then cull it. Purchasing quality beads that are more uniform in shape will enhance the beadwork and make beading easier and faster by reducing the culling time. Some stitches, like peyote and square stitch are more sensitive to the differences in the bead dimensions. Fringe styles are also sensitive to this issue particularly standard fringe.

Half thread method

The Half Thread Method is based on two beading truths. One is that a short thread is easier to work with than a longer one. The other truth is that adding a new thread is tedious and laborious. With the Half Thread Method, you cut a thread that is twice as long so you eliminate the need to add thread. And, by using one half at a time, it is easier to work with than a longer thread. Begin by putting a stop bead in the middle of thread.

> **Tip**: The long tail thread can be trouble for some beaders. To alleviate this problem, simply take a sticky note and loosely wrap the thread around it. Continue wrapping the thread until it's close to the beadwork and fold the note in half with the sticky portion inside. The long tail thread will now be easy to handle while you are working with the needle thread. When you are ready to use the tail thread, open the sticky notes and un-wrap the thread.

You will be beading from the middle of the beadwork toward one end. Continue until instructed to stop. Next, remove the stop bead, put a needle on that thread end and continue beading from the middle of the beadwork to the other end. This is especially useful when creating fringe. Use a long length of thread (typically 6 yards) and start in the center. Leave a 3 yard tail (use 1/2 of the thread) and create all of the fringes to the right with the needle thread end. Finally, remove the stop bead from the tail thread, add a needle and stitch all the fringes to the left.

Add a Stop bead

Starting a project of beadwork often involves leaving the tail thread for use later in completing the beadwork. Accordingly, there are no beginning knots to hold the tension. The use of a "Stop Bead" compensates for this and helps to hold the tension in the thread. The stop bead is a bead that is used temporarily and is removed later.

To add a stop bead, pick up the stop bead. Move it to the desired location and stitch through it again so the thread is looped around the bead. Be careful not to stitch through the thread inside the bead since that will cause problems when you try to remove it later. Pull the thread so the loop is tightly around the bead.

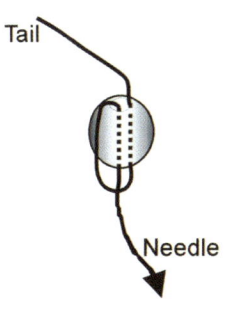

> **Tip**: The best stop bead is a size 8 or 9 bead in a matte finish because the roughness of the matte finish helps to hold the thread better and it is a large enough bead to easily remove later.

Ladder Stitch –

Basic 2-bead Ladder Stitch:

1. Cut 1 1/2 yards of thread and put a needle on to work single thread. Add a stop bead with a nine inch tail.

2. Pick up four seed beads and move to the stop bead. Stitch through the first two beads again and pull to create two columns. Then stitch through the last column.

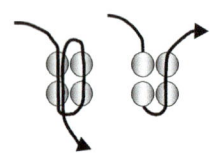

3. Pick up two seed beads. Stitch through the previous column and then through the added column.

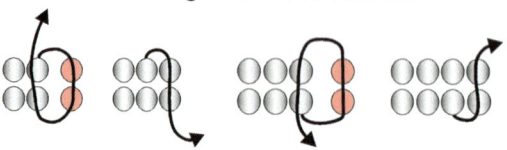

> **Tip**: Don't worry if your ladder strip looks a little wonky because the columns are not perfectly straight up and down next to each other. Notice that the top of the ladder has two threads on one intersection alternating with one thread on the next. However, Step 5 below "fixes" that by weaving back through the strip which will add a second thread to the intersections with one and will straighten up the columns.

4. Repeat step 3 until you have the desired number of columns.

5. Stitch back through the ladder strip to return to the second column in the strip. Remove the stop bead. Use the tail thread and needle thread to tie a square knot. Weave in the ends and cut.

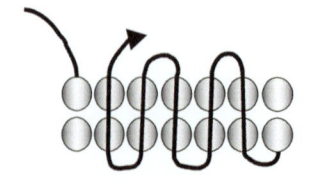

> **Tip**: Many experienced beaders will tie the knots and leave the weaving in of the end threads until the last step of the project. This helps ensure that bead holes will not already be filled with thread as you create the project. You can cut the thread ends to six inches or wrap in folded sticky note paper to reduce the annoyance of the thread ends as you work

Basic 1-bead Ladder Stitch:

Use the instructions for the Basic 2-bead Ladder Stitch except pick up half the number of beads.

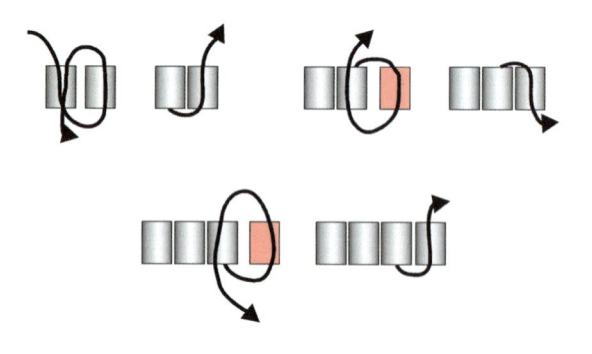

Basic 3-bead Ladder Stitch:

Use the instructions for the Basic 2-bead Ladder Stitch except pick up three beads for every two.

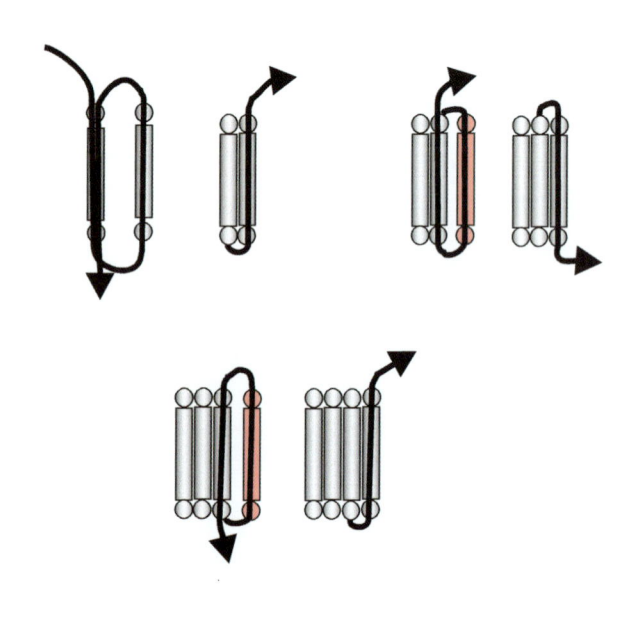

Ladder Stitch with Windows:

The previous basic ladder stitches utilized only the ladder columns (the steps of the ladder). This stitch can also be performed with beads in between the steps (the sides of the ladder) creating windows. Use the instructions for the Basic 2-bead Ladder Stitch except pick up beads for the sides in addition to the steps.

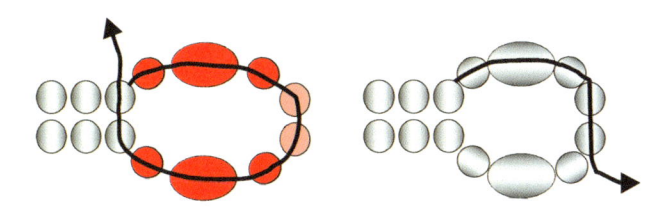

And, the top and bottom beads can be different.

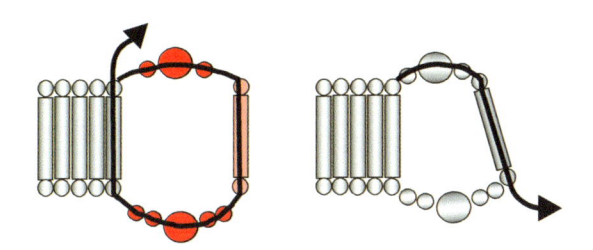

Stringing with Flexible beading wire:

1. String one crimp bead and nine 11/0 beads.

2. Put the end through the crimp bead and adjust the tension. Crimp the crimp bead and trim the end.

3. String the beads according to the bead chart, starting and ending with a 6/0 bead.

4. Repeat steps 1 and 2. Be sure to adjust the tension in both the bead strand and in the loop before crimping.

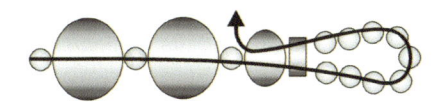

5. Finish with Findings, page 90.

Stringing with Thread

1. Add a stop bead leaving a six inch tail.

2. String the beads according to the instructions starting and ending with a 6/0 bead.

3. Pick up nine 11/0 beads and move down to the stand. Stitch through the beads again and pull to create a loop.

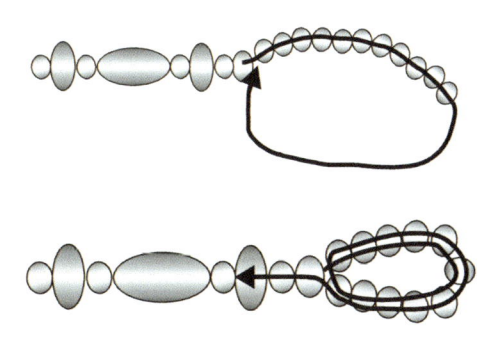

4. Stitch back through the bead strand to the starting point and remove the stop bead. Repeat step 3 being careful to pull the thread so the loop is positioned next to the bead strand. Use the needle and tail threads to tie a square knot plus.

5. Put a needle on the tail thread(s) and stitch down the strand two inches. Use the needle thread to stitch around the loop one more time, then stitch down the strand two inches. Cut the threads next to the beads.

6. Finish with Findings, page 90.

Necklace strand with side attachment:

1. Cut 2 yards of thread and put a needle on. Move the needle to the center to work with doubled thread. Add a stop bead leaving a six inch tail and string the beads according to the instructions starting with a 6/0 bead.

2. Pick up three 11/0 beads and stitch into the last column of the beadwork. Pick up three 11/0 beads and stitch back through the bead strand.

3. Do steps 3 through 5 "Stringing with thread" above.

4. Finish with Findings (page 90).

Finish with Findings:

The projects all use the same basic design technique which is to create a beaded loop to attach the clasp findings. This methodology allows for maximum flexibility; broken findings can be easily replaced, the type of closure, including the color and size can be changed at any time. My favorite necklace closure is a hook on one side and a length of chain on the other. This provides for easy adjustment of the length either to adjust the size for different people or for personal preferences about necklace lengths. When your clothing changes, from an open neckline to a turtle neck, you can easily change how the necklace fits. The standard necklace kit includes a head pin. String a couple of beads used in the necklace on the head pin, trim and loop it on the end of the chain for a professional finish.

The instructions for bracelets also use this methodology, and it is not just because I love shopping for clasps! I do this for the same reasons as discussed for necklaces and it is even more important with bracelets for several reasons.

* The stress and knocking on a bracelet clasp is more than any other finding gets, so, the chance for the clasp to break is greater. When the clasp is attached with jump rings, any breakage is easily solved by simply opening the jump rings and attaching a new clasp.

* Many people have strong opinions concerning the use of silver or gold color for their jewelry. If the clasp is attached with jump rings, you can easily switch from gold to silver or vice versa so the bracelet works best for them.

* Bracelets need to be different lengths to fit different people (not all wrists are the same size). You can easily re-size a bracelet when the clasp is attached by jump rings. You can change the style or type of clasp to make it smaller or larger. You can add more jump rings or beads between the loop and the clasp to make it larger. Each of these methods will change the length and therefore the fit of the bracelet. One quarter inch is a major change in a bracelet size so this is an important design point to consider. I generally create bracelets for a small size and use these techniques to make it larger if needed.

Steps:

1. Use pliers to open a jump ring by twisting open. Do not open by spreading the ends outward and enlarging the circle; you'll weaken the ring and destroy the roundness. Instead, using a pair of pliers in each hand, twist the ring open pushing one end forward and the other end backward. Insert the jump ring through the beaded loop and the finding. Close the jump ring reversing the twist done to open it. If possible, put two jump rings on each attachment area. This provides the same strength as a split ring but is easier to use and is more attractive and decorative than using one jump ring.

2. Repeat step 1 in each loop area.

3. For necklaces, add a few of the necklace beads on a headpin. Use wire cutters to trim and round nose pliers to create an end loop on the head pin. Twist the end loop around the bottom end of the chain.

Knots -

Knots are used at the end of stitching to secure threads before they are cut. There are two situations for knots. One is when two thread ends are available to perform a knot, the other is when only one thread is available.

Square Knot and Square Knot Plus

Use this knot whenever there are two threads available to tie the knot. When a square knot is knotted correctly and woven into the beadwork in opposite directions then any stress on the knot actually makes it tighter.

1. Position the thread ends so that they are exiting two different beads. One thread is on the right and the other is on the left. (figure 1)

2. Loop the right over and around the left. Pull the threads to position the knot. (figure 2) Then take the thread that is now on the left and loop it over and around the right. (figure 3) Pull the ends to secure the knot. (figure 4) This is a **square knot.**

5. Skip this step for a square knot, execute for **Square Knot Plus**. Take the thread on the right and loop it over and around the thread on the left. Pull both ends tightly.

6. Take one end and weave into the beadwork in one direction. Take the other end and weave into the beadwork in the opposite direction (see Weaving into Beadwork) then cut.

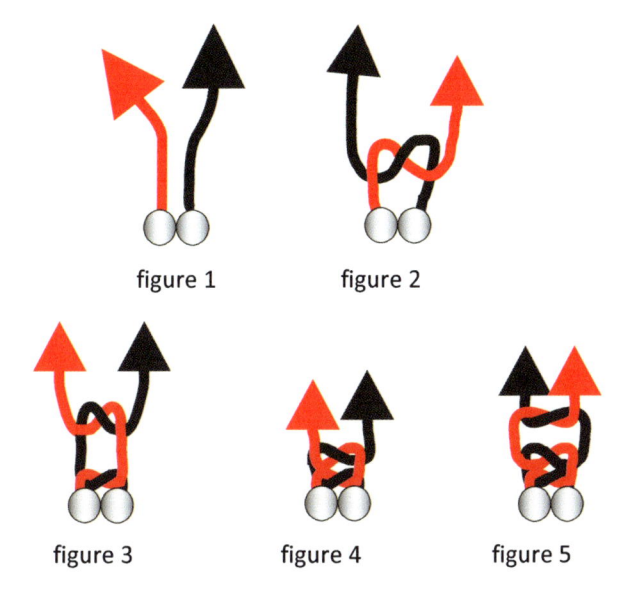

figure 1

figure 2

figure 3

figure 4

figure 5

One-Thread Knot

1. Stitch to an area in the beadwork where there are two threads coming out of a bead into two different directions. Stitch under the two threads and create pull gently to create a loop. Or, if on a backing, stitch through the fabric to create a loop.

2. Stitch through the loop, then through the loop again.

3. Pull slowly to close the loops. Pull tight.

4. Weave the thread into the beadwork (see below), then cut.

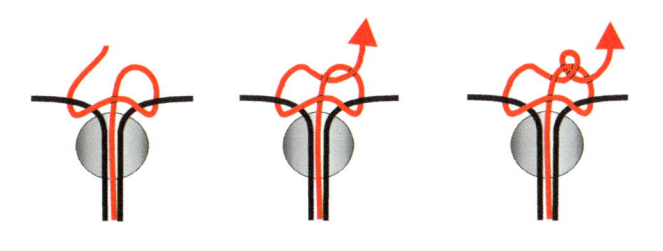

Half-Hitch Knot

Perform just like the one thread knot, except on step 2, and stitch through the loop only once.

Weaving into beadwork

Weave thread ends into the beadwork before cutting the thread; do not cut near the knot. Fabric weavers have discovered that weaving threads back in, actually eliminates the need for knots if the weaving is done up then down then up then down. Weaving done in this back and forth pattern will secure the thread without the need for a knot. So, knot AND weave to produce a really secure thread end.

Standard beading kit:
Size 12 beading needle, 2 inch length
Nymo, Silamide, or similar type thread, size B
Scissors
Bead Mat

Selecting a thread color to use for any beading project is a designer choice. Even though most threads are available in many colors so you can match the thread color to the main color in the beadwork, some beaders use only two colors; a light grey (as the neutral) and black for projects with dark beads. I prefer to first look at the type of beads that are being used. If there are transparent beads, then I look at the lightest color beads to dictate my thread color. When beads are a light color and are transparent, you can see the thread through the beads so the color of thread affects the final appearance of the bead. I select a thread color that will not alter the color of those beads. After the project is finished, if there are areas where a light color thread is exposed around dark colored beads, use a fine tip permanent marker to color those thread areas. If there are no transparent beads, select any color of thread.

Standard Necklace kit:
2 each seed beads 6/0 in color to match necklace beads
4 each 5mm round jump rings
1 each hook
4 inches chain, at least 5mm links
1 each 2 inch head pin
Round nose pliers
Flat nose pliers

Substitution:
The most common size seed bead is size 11/0. If a project calls for a size 11/0 seed bead, substitution with another size bead is not recommended. However, feel free to substitute the following sizes in all the projects:

Size 14/0 with 15/0 and vice versa.
Size 8/0 with 9/0 and vice versa.
Size 5/0 with 6/0 and vice versa.

Conversion Chart:
1 inch = 2.54 centimeters (cm)
1 foot = 0.3048 meters (m)
1 yard = 3 feet
1 yard = 0.91440 meters (m)
1 gram = 0.035274 ounces (oz)

Terminology:
Core: The center/main strand for branch fringe and spiral fringe.

Decrease/Increase: The amount of change in the standard count of seed beads from one fringe to the next.

End sequence: The group of other beads at the bottom of fringe after the standard count of seed beads.

Count: The number of seed beads to pick up before the end sequence of fringe.

End bead(s): The bead(s) at the bottom of the fringe that hold the fringe beads on the strand.

Gallery: by Jamie Cloud Eakin

Index

Attaching to beadwork	12
Bracelets	34,44,58
Branch fringe	60
Circles branch fringe	63
Conversion chart	92
Earrings	32,33,50,72,85
Half thread method	87
Kinky fringe	52
Knots	91
Ladder stitch	88
Leaf end	11
Loop branch fringe	63
Loop end	11
Loop fringe	36
Necklaces	20,22,24,27,28, 30,40,43,46,48, 56,66,68,69,74, 76,78,81,84
Picot end	10
Pins	53,74
Ribbon spiral fringe	83
Shorthand-Branch fringe	64
Shorthand-Kinky fringe	53
Spiral fringe	80
Standard fringe	15
Standard kits	92
Star end	10
Stop bead	87
Substitution	92
Terminology	92
Turn bead	10
Twisted fringe	77

Gallery: by Jamie Cloud Eakin

Acknowledgements:

All creative people know the "birth pains" associated with the creative process and the people around them experience this as well! I want to thank all those who suffered with me, encouraged me and had to endure the highs and lows that inevitably occur. So... Stephen, Candace, Sis, Yvonne, Pam, Lee please know I appreciate your support and love. There are others too (and you know who you are). Let me just say with a loud and heart felt shout "Thank you!"

About the Author:

Jamie Cloud Eakin has been a professional bead artist for over two decades, and she teaches and sells her work in galleries across North America. She is the author of Beading with Cabochons (Lark 2005) and Bugle Bead Bonanza (Lark 2010), Dimensional Bead Embroidery (Lark 2011) and Bead Embroidery Jewelry Projects (Lark 2013). Jamie lives in Modesto, California. Her website is www.StudioJamie.com.

Gallery: by Jamie Cloud Eakin

Gallery: by Jamie Cloud Eakin

Printed in Great Britain
by Amazon